Journey into a
GREATER
Concern

Stepping into the journey of God's plan for your life

SCOTT LACKEY

Journey into a **GREATER** Concern
by SCOTT LACKEY

Published by:

LAMP POST
publishers

www.lamppostpublishers.com

Trade Paperback: ISBN-13 # 978-1-60039-128-6
ebook: ISBN-13 # 978-1-60039-129-3

CONTENTS

Journey into a
GREATER
Concern

ONE

The Journey

In November of 2017, Netflix released *Jim and Andy: The Great Beyond*, a documentary about Jim Carrey's portrayal of the late comedian Andy Kaufman in the 1999 movie *Man on the Moon*. Full of behind-the-scenes footage, it consists mostly of Carrey reminiscing about his experience on the set playing Kaufman. If you're not familiar with Andy Kaufman, he is potentially one of the top five funniest people to ever live. If you have thirty minutes, head over to YouTube and type in "Andy Kaufman." Just watch. You will either love him, hate him, or say "What Just happened?" or maybe all three.

In the documentary, Carrey talks about his childhood, his years in standup, his career in general, and how everything essentially came to a climax in this role as Andy Kaufman. At one point, while talking about his standup career (and in some ways correlating it to Andy's), Carrey describes an epiphany he had while developing his act. He shared that one night he woke up and realized that his role as a stand-up was to take the audience to a place where they are "free from concern."[1] That statement blew my mind. I have watched the documentary several times, and every time I hear it my response is the same: "Wow!"

I want to be free from concern, *you* want to be free from concern, *we all* would like to, in some way, be free from concern. Whenever I see Jim Carrey in *Ace Ventura, Dumb & Dumber, LiarLiar*, and yes, even *The Cable Guy*, I'm brought to a moment where I'm free from concern. Comedy has a way of doing that. A moment of laughter takes our soul to a place where we forget about all of the stresses of life that bring us into concern.

Let's jump over to Jerry Seinfeld's latest standup special, *23 Hours to Kill,* which was released on Netflix in May 2020. Jerry begins his act by telling a joke about how nobody really wants to be where they currently are (physically speaking). Seinfeld, in his humorous way, makes the contention that everyone is getting to one place just so they can be concerned about getting to the next place. We as humans don't always know to embrace the moment; we are always concerned about what is next. Seinfeld, in his own unique method, is saying the same thing as Jim Carrey: we want to be free of the concern that constantly nags at our minds, but we cannot seem to free ourselves of it. There is always "one more thing" to be concerned about.

---

1   *Jim and Andy the Great Beyond*, Netflix.

It seems as though we have this nagging feeling of concern all of the time. We want to be free from it but it so quickly weighs us down. I'm not fighting a war on "concern." Concern can be a very positive thing, it can be the very thing that empowers us to be responsible and *do something*. The problem is when our concern develops into worry. Or when our concern is actually just feeding our craving for control. Or when our concern is only focused on the small task that is coming next (as Seinfeld would contend). Short sighted and self-absorbed, we are never able to be concerned about others.

It would be nice to be free from concern, freeing ourselves up to become others focused. The items in the list below are not necessarily bad, but these small concerns can lead to worry, a desire for control (which we never actually have), and cause short-sightedness:

- Does my boss like me?
- When will he/she text me back?
- How many "likes" will my post get?
- How do I get noticed?
- How do I get more followers?
- Does my dog still like me?

And the list goes on and on... If you have allowed any of these concerns to control you, don't feel bad. We've all been there before.

Isn't it crazy how sometimes we can have a whole list of things to do, but we get so caught up waiting for someone to text or message us back on one item that we will hold off being productive on the other items on the list? Why is that? I have noticed that it derives from our self-centered, self-absorbed need for the affirmation of a response.

How do we get to a place where, though we are not completely free of concern, we can be free of petty concern? How do we get to a place where we can focus on the greater journey of our life, opposed to always just wanting to get to "what is next?" How do we develop a healthy level of concern that is not bogged down by worry, control, or short-sightedness?

These are the questions that I want us to take a deeper look at in the following pages. We are going to look at these questions through the life of a guy named Jacob. We find Jacob's story in the first book of the Old Testament: the Book of Genesis. Jacob is by no means a perfect person—in fact there are some very large blemishes on his life story. The journey of Jacob will show us how we can step into a healthy level of concern based upon a life "calling" instead of a concern based on the immediacy of "what's next?" Through the ups and downs of Jacob's life we will discover what it truly means to be on a journey, and how on our journey we can break away from self-centered concern.

"Then Jacob went on his *journey*, and came to
the land of the sons of the east" (Genesis 29:1).

Jacob's life journey is filled with wins and losses, victories and defeats, disappointments and blessings. We will witness his imperfections, his struggles and hang-ups. Yet we will see through the journey of Jacob that we have something—or someone—who can elevate our level of concern to such a place that our life journey becomes oriented around a sense of calling that is far beyond ourselves.

Now I know some of you reading this right now may be thinking:

"The Old Testament?"

"Genesis?"

"Isn't that dated information?"

According to an article released by Forbes,[2] as of July 2020 *The Office* has experienced more time in Netflix's Top 10 over the past five months than any other show or movie. Why bring this up? *The Office* came on air in 2005 and left the air in 2013. Technology has moved at such a rapid pace that many of the themes in the show are outdated. The characters don't even have smartphones in the first few seasons. Yet the show still resonates with people, and it still has messages that are deeply true about human relationships.

---

2   https://www.forbes.com/sites/travisbean/2020/07/24/25-most-popular-shows-netflix-2020/#28c5e02f44bd

I would make the same contention with the ancient stories of the Scriptures. Technologically speaking, and even at times socially speaking, they appear to be outdated, but the stories have deep truths that still speak to us today. I personally believe that all of these stories actually happened in history. You may disagree...that's okay. You can still learn a lot from the story of Jacob. The themes and the truths we discover in this journey, specifically as it relates to moving beyond a place of self-concern, are still deeply relevant.

What does it look like for us to journey through life on purpose? Let's challenge our self-concern and learn what it means to step into a greater concern. May we grow together through looking at the life of Jacob. We are not here by accident. Let's take this journey together to the place where we go beyond ourselves in pursuit of a greater concern!

TWO

You Set Yourself Up

When I was fifteen years old, I had the opportunity to help with a golf tournament fundraiser in a beautiful place called Ellicottville, NY. Ellicottville is a quaint little village in the Southern Tier of New York State, and is mostly known as being a ski and snowboard town in the winter. The particular incident I'm describing took place in the summertime. I was sitting at one of the golf holes with my friend, and we had the responsibility to briefly chat with the golfers and provide them with water. At one point one of the golf carts that came to our hole was being driven by a former quarterback for the Buffalo Bills. This particular quarterback is a legend in Buffalo—he went to four straight Super Bowls.

At this point in time I had never played golf in my life. My golf experience consisted of a few games of miniature golf, and I was horrendous even at that. For some reason I decided rather boldly to suggest which club this former Buffalo Bills quarterback should use on this hole.

In response, he quickly pulled $200 out of his pocket and said, "I will give you this $200 if you can get the ball on the green with that club." I had to try. What did I have to lose? I went up to the hole and while I was attempting to practice my swing, he yelled, "Look at that sugar-britches trying to hit a golf ball." I swung, and I hit the ball! And it rolled forward only a few feet. For the rest of the summer, many of my co-workers referred to me as "sugar-britches." I was not proud of this name, BUT *I set myself up*. I knew absolutely nothing about golf, but for some reason I decided I was going to give someone advice about how to play it. Definitely *not* one of my proudest moments. This is a silly, momentary example, but unfortunately this reality plays itself out in life as a whole. *How often do we set ourselves up for the journey that our life is on?*

As we go on the journey of life we have to recognize that some of the things that happen to us are a result of our setting ourselves up. Your boss has been treating you poorly. How have you been treating your boss? Your spouse has been short with you lately. How have you been showing love and affection toward your spouse? Your best friend appears to be more distant than normal. What consistent efforts have you made to draw close to that person? You feel lonely. Are you spending more time in front of a screen than pursuing real relationships with real people? These things don't always correlate, but there are times when the above examples would be appropriate questions to ask. We have a responsibility to look in the mirror.

JACOB MEETS LABAN

And this is where we find our friend Jacob. In Genesis 29, Jacob is heading out on his journey. In Genesis 28, Jacob experienced God in a dream and God told him, "I am with you and will keep you wherever you go, and will bring you back to this land; for I will not leave you until I have done what I have promised you."[3] We will come to find later that this is a very loaded statement. On one hand, if you are Jacob you would find great peace in knowing that God will be with you as set out on your new journey. On the other hand, the thought of going back to where you came from does not appear to be a viable option, especially considering what Jacob had done (we will explore Jacob's past soon).

Jacob is on a journey to find his Uncle Laban and stay with him. Jacob find's Laban's daughter Rachel, and Rachel relays the message to her father. "So when Laban heard the news of Jacob his sister's son, he ran to meet him, and embraced him and kissed him and brought him to his house."[4] This seems great! Jacob went on a journey to find his uncle and they are together, hugging, and hanging out

---

3   Genesis 28:15
4   Genesis 29:13

at Laban's house. Jacob is at the part of his journey where things could seemingly end, but there is much more to come.[5]

LABAN TRICKS JACOB

Jacob is enamored with Laban's daughter Rachel. In his mind he is probably thinking, "It will be easy for me to get Rachel. She likes me, I like her, her dad likes me, and on top of all of that, God told me that he is with me wherever I go. How could anything possibly go wrong?" Jacob makes a deal with Laban that he will work for him for seven years so that he can marry Rachel. "So Jacob served seven years for Rachel and they seemed to but a few days because of his love for her."[6] What a great guy! Working hard to marry the love of his life. Romance, passion, it's a beautiful story! That is...until the wedding night.

Rachel had an older sister named Leah. From what the author of Genesis tells us, Leah is not as physically attractive

---

5   *Spoiler Alert*: Jacob is about to work for his uncle and marry two of his uncle's daughters. Keep in mind that this was a *different time* and *different culture*. This book is not a book about incest or polygamy. As you read the story you will also notice that this is not your traditional modern western story of two people who find true love and find a way to get married. Jacob works for Laban for seven years so that he can marry one of his daughters. This is a different time, therefore there is a different context. If you want to know more of the context I would highly recommend *The NIV Application Commentary: Genesis* by John H. Walton.

6   Genesis 29:20

as Rachel. Laban promised Rachel to be Jacob's wife, but instead something else happens. It's night time. Jacob is ready (if you know what I mean). And Jacob and Rachel... let's just say they "get down to *business*." Unfortunately for Jacob, he discovers the next morning that he wasn't doing *business* with Rachel. Jacob conducted *business*, to be sure, but that *business* was transacted with Leah!

Jacob asks Laban how this happened. Laban explains that Leah is the older sister, and it is customary for the older sister to get married first. But Jacob was in love with Rachel! So Laban allowed Jacob to marry her as well—in exchange for another seven years of work for Laban. By the end of this whole affair, Jacob has worked for fourteen years and has two wives.

In his time on Laban's property Jacob becomes a father to children through both Leah and Rachel. Laban's flocks begin to prosper, and he recognizes that this prosperity is a result of the favor of God on Jacob's life (Genesis 30:27). Jacob eventually departs from Laban (we will return to this), but before we look at that we must address a staggering truth. Jacob ultimately spends twenty years of his life working for Laban. *Twenty years! Two decades!* Think of all that you can accomplish in twenty years. And it all began when Laban tricked Jacob into staying the first seven years with the promise of Rachel but giving him Leah instead.

How did this happen? Well in some ways Jacob *set himself up*. Jacob himself was a manipulator. Jacob loved controlling the narrative. This isn't karma (I don't subscribe to that), this has to do with Jacob's view on the world, and his view of people. Jacob viewed people (especially his brother Esau) as resources to control and steal from as opposed to image-bearers of God who have inherent value. This is how most manipulators view people—as resources to help fulfill their own selfish agenda. If you play this game long enough, you will eventually meet another manipulator who will out manipulate you. Once again, this isn't karma, but instead it's a demonstration that like-minded people are attracted to one another. Jacob *set himself up*.

JACOB'S PAST

Jacob's past is ultimately what set him for this opportunity to be used by Laban. Jacob had a history of using others, specifically his brother Esau. Esau and Jacob were twins, but Esau was the older of the two. Esau is described as a rough, hairy man who liked to hunt, while Jacob is depicted as softer—smooth skinned—more interested in cooking, and possibly a little more sophisticated. Esau definitely had the physical advantage. But Jacob, preferring to engage in a battle of the wits, found a way to take two critical things from his brother: the birthright and the blessing.

In Genesis 25 we read that one day Esau was starving after working in the field. Jacob is making stew and he tells Esau that he can have some if Esau will give him his birthright. Now, Esau is either about to legitimately starve to death, or more likely, he is being a bit dramatic, perhaps a little "hangry." So he gives in and surrenders his birthright to Jacob for a bowl of stew. This was a big deal.[7] This means that Jacob would receive two-thirds of the inheritance. I have always wondered: Could Esau actually not find any food elsewhere? Or since he was physically stronger, why didn't he just punch his brother in the face and take the stew?

Jacob had successfully stolen the birthright, and in Genesis 27 he is ready to take the blessing as well. Isaac (Jacob and Esau's dad) is aging, he can't see very well, and he is fragile. Isaac is ready to bless Esau, so he sends Esau out to hunt and make him a meal. Following the meal, Isaac will bless Esau. Rebekah (their mother) favors Jacob over Esau, and she overheard Isaac sending Esau out. Rebekah desires for Jacob to have the blessing, so she comes up with a plan.

Remember: Isaac cannot see very well. Rebekah makes a delicious meal, put's Esau's clothes on Jacob, and covers his hands in goatskins. Dressed as Esau, Jacob brings the meal to his father, Isaac. Isaac recognizes that Jacob's voice

---

7   "The birthright was the oldest son's share of the material estate of the family. In the ancient world the firstborn typically received a double share of the inheritance. Thus, if there were twelve sons, the inheritance would be divided into thirteen and the oldest would receive two-thirteenths. In other words, the fewer the number of sons the greater the discrepancy. In the case of Jacob and Esau, the inheritance would someday be divided into three parts, and Esau would receive two-thirds—twice of what Jacob would receive" (John Walton, *NIV Application Commentary*, pg.554).

doesn't sound like Esau, but when he feel's the hair on Jacob's hands he is convinced. Isaac moves forward and blesses Jacob. Jacob now has the blessing from God that is passed down from one generation to the next.

When Esau returns, he discovers the blessing has been given to Jacob. Isaac is upset. Esau is upset. He plots to kill his brother over this deception. The story of this dysfunctional family raises to such an extreme level that Rebekah compels Jacob to run away from home to his uncle Laban.

YOU WILL NOT SEE LABAN COMING

When you live the way Jacob lived in his early life, you will not see Laban coming. The man who seems to be a blessing, offering new opportunity and a beautiful daughter, actually controls Jacob's life for twenty years. *I cannot reiterate enough, Jacob set himself up.* This is the ultimate issue with inward-focused self-concern. You will not see Laban coming to play the same trick on you that you played on others. Because you are only thinking about yourself, you can not see the bigger picture, and your perspective remains short-sighted and self-centered.

The manipulator becomes the manipulated. Why? Because you won't see it coming. Not only will you not see it coming, but it may be your only option. Jacob had nowhere else to go, he had burned the relational bridges with his brother by his manipulation. His self-centered motives had left him with nowhere else to turn.

This is a great challenge for us: To ask the Spirit of God to check our motives in all things. If we don't check our motives regarding others, we may find ourselves in the same place as Jacob: manipulated, trapped, nowhere else to go.

What is your view of people? Jacob saw his brother as nothing more than a *means to an end.* Laban viewed Jacob with the same opportunistic attitude. Manipulative self-concern robs us of true productive relationships because people are simply a *means* to our own personal *end.* This brings us to a critical question that we all must ask ourselves: "How do I view other people?" The people in your life are not a *means* to service your *end* goal for your own fulfillment. Below are the downfalls of viewing people in this manner:

1. We dehumanize others instead of seeing them as image bearers of God.

2. We see others as servants for our benefit, not as people to be served.

3. We create a cycle of stress-filled concern, always wondering, "How do I get an edge?"

4. We find ourselves always looking over our shoulders for those we have manipulated. (I imagine Jacob often wondered, "When is Esau going to find me and kill me?")

5. Eventually someone will come along who is much better at this game than you are and they will outsmart you at your game.

In the New Testament Book of Galatians, the apostle Paul writes, "Let us not lose heart in doing good, for in due time we will reap if we do not grow weary."[8] The inverse of this is true as well. We will reap whatever it is that we sow. If we sow seeds of controlling others, we will eventually be controlled by others. If we sow seeds of working for the good of others, we will see a harvest of goodness that comes as a result. Why do we allow ourselves to get caught up in such a destructive cycle when we have been given the option to work for the good?

The most healthy perspective is to see every human we interact with as someone who reflects the image of God. That means that every person has *value* no matter their background, social status, race, attitude, or personality. *Everyone* is created in God's image—including you! And you, as an image bearer, have something of value to add to people's lives, and all of the people around you have something valuable to add to your life as well. (*Yes, even that guy at work who obnoxiously chews with his mouth open every day at lunch has something valuable to add.*) We don't extract the value out of others for our own personal gain,

---

8   Galatians 6:9

but instead we work together to accomplish "good" things together, understanding that the value that we all have allows us to accomplish much greater things together than we ever could apart. This perspective allows us to step out of the realm of our own self-concern, and instead allows us to work together with others to take on much greater concerns that make a difference in the world. Together we can work for what is good.

LOSE YOUR LIFE

There is one more—maybe even more important—perspective shift that must be made in order for us to work toward that which is good. We are living in a different time in history than Isaac, Rebekah, Jacob, Esau, Laban, Rachel, and Leah, and we should rejoice in that for many reasons. The predominant reason for that is because we live in a post-resurrection world. In the world of Jacob, Jesus had not yet come. Jesus is the image of the invisible God. That means for us Jesus is the perfect picture of what true humanity looks like. Do you want to know how you can work for what is good? Look at the life, teaching, and ministry of Jesus, you will very quickly see how your life can work for what is good.

But...

Let's take it one more step.

This next step.

This question.

Changes everything.

Do you believe that you truly find life when you lose your life?

Think about that question. Stop reading. Really think about it.

This is what Jesus teaches, "For whoever wishes to save his life will lose it; but whoever loses his life for My sake will find it."[9] True life is found when we lay down our life and step into the journey and step into the story that Jesus has for us. True life is found when we lose our life. Laying down our purposes and pursuing a greater purpose that we have been created for.

When we lose our life for the life Jesus called us to, we step into a life of love. A life that is not about us, but about others. "Greater love has no one than this, that one lay down his life for his friends."[10] This place of being free from self-concern and working from a place for the good of others—this is a concern of love, continually laying down our life so that others may have life. This is the upward call, this is what we have been created for.

Are you ready to lose your life so that others may find the one who *is* life?

Are you ready to lay down your personal concern and live for the concern of others?

---

9   Matthew 16:25

10   John 15:13

Are you ready to step into a place where you value others above yourself?

Are you ready to work toward that which is good?

Let's say "yes" to these challenges, not because of religious obligation but because we are motivated by love, because we are following the way of Jesus who laid down his life so that others could have life. May we look beyond ourselves and work together to do the same. Just like Jacob, you are *setting yourself up* for the future with your actions in the present.

Are you *setting yourself up* to work for the good of others?

Or...

Are you *setting yourself up* to be controlled by others?

THREE

Experience and Potential

If you ever happen to hear me sing, all I can say is that I'm sorry. I'm literally tone deaf. I will never understand how I made it into my elementary school choir, and I will never forget how the kids who stood next to me would tell me to sing more quietly because I was throwing off their pitch. In the middle of fifth grade, my elementary school choir career came to an end—but not because of my inability to sing. The teacher and I didn't quite see eye to eye. Did I view choir practice as an opportunity to create some type of personal comedy stage? Yes. Yes I did! Did my behavior necessitate our choir director telling my friend in front of the entire class that she was ashamed of him for hanging out with me and that I was going to lead him down the wrong path? Possibly. Definitely maybe. But that was probably a little extreme, right?

After that incident, the tension between myself and my choir teacher continued to rise. I knew that my days in the choir were numbered. I just needed a way out. I talked to my mother and she told me that I could drop out of choir if I went and talked to the choir teacher myself. This was nerve wracking. I was a fifth grader and I had to go tell an adult why I no longer wanted to be in her choir. I got to school early that day, walked to her room, and through some stammering I broke the news to her. I stated my issues with her for publicly calling me out. She did not apologize, and she did not try to convince me to stay. When the conversation was over, I felt very relieved. I was ready for a new, post-choir life. But I could tell in my heart that this would not be the end of difficult conversations in my life. This was my first step in learning how to speak up for myself and handle conflict. This was a new experience, but a preparatory one.

When I was in ninth grade I remember the principal of my high school calling my mother and informing her that I was "leading a mutiny" in my English class. Was this true? Most definitely. Was it absolutely hilarious? Mostly. Was it highly disrespectful and inappropriate? Emphatically yes. As much as my behavior was out of hand, I will never forget when I felt I was given that label "leader." Even though it was in a negative light, it still felt like a badge of honor—a highlight of potential—of what *could* happen with my life.

The experience of confronting my choir teacher, along with the potential of the label "leader," were two very specific things that were a foreshadowing of my future.

Call it divine intervention, the cosmos aligning, or just pure happenstance. I have often found that when we own our past experiences and own the labels of potential that we have been given, those things tend to become a foreshadowing of what is to come. We just have to remember that these experiences are preparing us for an even *more difficult* experience.

As I have grown into adulthood...I HATE conflict. Every time that I know I'm about to step into a difficult conversation I begin to stress out about it. But guess what gives me confidence when I'm stepping into a conflict-conversation? My past experience—and it all started with the time I confronted my choir teacher. When a pending conversation carries the illusion of greater difficulty, my past experiences become an affirmation that I can handle what is next. I'm only in my late twenties and I have already had to confront people in some very strenuous circumstances. If my experiences are in some way preparing me for managing future conflict, I can't imagine what still must be to come!

Potential works in a similar fashion. But while our past circumstances provide us experiences that show what we can do, the potential others see in us provide us inspiration for what we can become. The potential of a label like "leader" is a captivating thing to pursue. When I was given the label "leader" by the principal of my high school in my freshman year—even though it wasn't stated positively—I was given a type of potential to pursue. We are honored when we are given an admirable label to pursue, but we often forget the difficulty that comes through pursuing those labels. Maybe you're pursuing a label like:

- Leader
- Coach
- Doctor
- Pastor
- Husband
- Wife
- Parent
- Friend
- Confidant
- Courageous
- Achiever
- Entrepreneur
- Athlete

There is an endless list of admirable labels to pursue in this journey of life. The truth is that the potential for these labels is possible, but the question we must ask ourselves is: What are we clinging to when that potential is threatened? To truly pursue your potential, there will be bumps in the road. We are reminded of those bumps from that great philosopher—Rocky Balboa:

"Let me tell you something you already know. The world ain't all sunshine and rainbows. It's a very mean and nasty place and I don't care how tough you are. It will beat you to your knees and keep you there permanently if you let it. You, me, or nobody is gonna hit as hard as life. But it ain't about how hard ya hit. It's about how hard you can get hit and keep moving forward."[11]

It won't always be easy to move forward in life. We must have something to cling to. Defining moments in our past experiences give us a foreshadowing of our future. The potential within the labels we are given and pursue offer a foreshadowing of our future as well. What can we cling to that will allow us to step into the future that our *past experiences* and our *potential labels* are speaking to?

BEFORE THE JOURNEY

Remember where we started with Jacob in Chapter One? "Then Jacob went on his journey."[12] As we discovered in the last chapter, because of his personal choices and the serious family drama he caused, Jacob *set himself up* to have to run for his life, and he flees to a place called Bethel. But before his journey begins, Jacob has an *experience* in a dream where

---

11 *Rocky Balboa*, 2006.

12 Genesis 29:1

he encounters God. The dream is actually really cool: Jacob sees a ladder connecting heaven and earth with angels—this dream is wild! But I want to focus on something God says to Jacob in the dream, along with Jacob's response.

> **God:** Behold, I am with you and will keep you wherever you go, and *will bring you back to this land*; for I will not leave you until I have done what I have promised you.

(After Jacob wakes up from his dream, he sets up a memorial in order to remember it. Jacob calls the place Bethel, which means "House of God".)

> **Jacob:** "If God will be with me and will keep me on this journey that I take, and will give me food to eat and garments to wear, and I return to my father's house in safety, then the Lord will be my God. This stone, which I have set up as a pillar, will be God's house, and of all that You give me I will surely give a tenth to You."[13]

Jacob has an *experience* with God. The experience with God comes with a promise from God that speaks to Jacob's

---

13 Genesis 28:15-22

potential. For Jacob to grow into the potential label that he will one day receive from God (*Israel*), he will be required one day to follow the path of God to return to the land.

The journey into potential can be intimidating. God promises to bring Jacob back to his homeland. How? Not really sure. Remember Jacob is no longer welcome (his brother still lives there). But Jacob takes God at his word and believes that he will, in fact, one day return in safety. What could possibly make someone like Jacob want to return to such a predictable and potentially hostile situation? Perhaps by spending twenty years working for someone who continually over promised and under-delivered—like Laban?

More importantly, what could possibly give Jacob the confidence to break free from Laban? Perhaps *experience* with God and the *potential* of a promise from God.

ANOTHER SIDE OF CONTROL

It has now been twenty years since Jacob had that *experience* with God, along with receiving the *potential* of a promise from God. Laban's sons are not really fond of Jacob, and Jacob has had enough of Laban (can you blame him?). Jacob is ready to move on, so he says to Laban, "Send me away, that I may go to my own place and to my own country."[14] Laban attempts to convince Jacob to stay

---

14 Genesis 30:25b

by making a not-so-good deal, because Laban knows that he is receiving a blessing from God simply by having Jacob being around. But good deal or not, Jacob knows his time with Laban is up and it's time to go. God speaks clearly to Jacob:

> "...for I have seen all that Laban has been doing to you. I am the God of Bethel, where you anointed a pillar, where you made a vow to Me; now arise, leave this land, and return to the land of your birth."[15]

This seems easy enough. Twenty years under constant manipulation from Laban made it clear it was time for Jacob to move forward in his journey—but not so fast. For Jacob to move forward, he had to go back. The idea of leaving Laban seemed easy, but what was he leaving Laban for? And on top of that, Jacob had two wives and their children who he was now responsible for. From Genesis 32, we know that Jacob is "afraid and distressed"[16] to see Esau again. The tension is all too real.

Enter another side of control. In some ways, Laban *helped* Jacob. Laban allowed Jacob to marry two of his daughters, he provided Jacob with work, food, and a good

---

15 Genesis 31:12b-13
16 Genesis 32:7

lifestyle. *Does the benefit of Laban in Jacob's life outweigh the manipulation of Laban in Jacob's life?* Laban is representative of something or someone that is far too real in our lives. Laban was controlling Jacob. Laban was also providing protection for Jacob by making it easy to avoid confronting his past, and with it, his brother, Esau.

What do you do when that which controls you is also protecting you?

Now that's a tough one.

No easy answers here.

I remember the first time I felt that I was in this predicament. I was working in ministry. I felt *called* to ministry. I was living "the dream." Now, this dream didn't involve a huge salary or nice cars, but it was the dream that God had placed on my heart. As I was working in this particular ministry I began to notice some integrity issues with leadership. I even confronted some of the issues, yet nobody with the power to make changes actually wanted to be a part of the solution. There were those with more influence or authority who affirmed the issues, but nobody wanted to do anything. I was at a crossroads.

This was supposed to be something good. Yet I was in a bad situation. How do I get out? My position in ministry had control over me because it provided a paycheck. This paycheck was my Laban—it was a form of protection for me. My paycheck ensured I could pay my bills. In addition, this ministry leader had influence. If I left at such a young age, would he just trash my name in the community? Was I actually in the wrong and being a foolish young person? So many questions running through my mind. That which controlled me was also, in some weird way, protecting me.

Think of all of the things that could potentially be controlling you and the illusion of protection that they offer:

- Abusive job situation vs. Paycheck
- Manipulative friend vs. Companionship
- Substance abuse vs. Comfort
- Bad spending habits vs. Keeping up with everyone else
- Loss of integrity in the workplace vs. Promotion or Affirmation

This is by no means an exhaustive list, but all of these situations are real forms of control that offer a semblance of protection. How do we get out? How do we break free? Sometimes these come into our life without our own choosing, sometimes they come into our life because of one bad decision after another. However you got here, the reality is that you probably don't want to stay there.

This brings us back to *experience* and *potential*. When it came to my situation at this particular ministry position, I had to rely on my past experience of confronting difficult situations to address the issues I was seeing. After

I had confronted the situation and nobody responded to take action, I had to make the difficult decision to leave. This was not an easy choice, but it spoke to my potential to be a leader. Leaders have to make difficult decisions—even when we don't fully know where the outcome will lead us.

Jacob had to do the same thing. Jacob had to lean on his *experience* and his *potential* that was given to him by God in Genesis 28. God told him he would return and God gave him favor to move forward. God gave favor to Jacob by visiting Laban and telling him not to harm Jacob: "God came to Laban the Aramean in a dream of the night and said to him, 'Be careful that you do not speak to Jacob either good or bad.'"[17] God has authority over *who* or *what* is controlling you! God has prepared you through your experience for this moment to move forward, and by the power of his Spirit he has placed the potential inside of you to lead you into a new season of your life! That which is controlling you *no longer has to control you*, but just like Jacob, you must remember the promises of God and move forward in those promises! *Your experiences and your potential will propel you forward when they are rooted in the promises of God over your life.* Seek to have an experience with God and get to know the promises of God so that you can move forward in the potential God has for you!

---

17 Genesis 31:24b

CONTROL WILL NOT GIVE UP EASILY

When I finally decided to leave the unhealthy ministry I was a part of, the decision was not easy. I was told that I wasn't seeing the bigger picture. I was too young. I was inexperienced. Some months after leaving, the person responsible for leading this ministry into a dark place began texting me and telling me that people were reaching out to him for a reference and he was unable to say good things about me. He was trying to control the narrative of my reputation. Following that, he sent someone on his staff to attempt to hire me back, promising that things would "be different". When you finally come to the place where you choose to step into freedom, that which was controlling you will not give up easily. If you have stepped out of a controlling situation before understanding the influence which that person or substance has over you, the attempt to bring you back under control is all too real.

This is where we find Jacob. Jacob has developed the courage to move on with his family. Jacob is afraid to face his brother Esau, but he knows that he can no longer live under the manipulative conditions of Laban. And concerned with how Laban will handle the news that he and his family and his flocks are leaving, Jacob chooses to simply pack up and go without saying "goodbye." When Laban discovers that Jacob has sneaked away, he decides to track him down.

Then Laban said to Jacob, "What have you done by deceiving me and carrying away my daughters like captives of the sword? Why did you flee secretly and deceive me, and did not tell me so that I might have sent you away with joy and with songs, with timbrel and with lyre; and did not allow me to kiss my sons and my daughters? Now you have done foolishly. It is in my power to do you harm, but the God of your father spoke to me last night, saying, 'Be careful not to speak either good or bad to Jacob.' Now you have indeed gone away because you longed greatly for your father's house..."[18]

Oh, Laban! He sounds so heroic. Laban wishes that he could have sent Jacob away properly—with joy, songs, timbrels, and kisses. And he is so very righteous he even expresses how he is obeying God's instructions as to how he should speak to Jacob. This is what control does. It becomes indignant and self-righteous. And as soon as you take your first step into freedom—whether it's a person or the thoughts within your own mind—control will seep back in and try to sell you a load of crap. I'm sorry, I know that's crass. But that's exactly what Laban did: After twenty years

---

18 Genesis 31:26-30

of manipulation, he is trying to make Jacob feel guilty. He is presenting himself as the injured party. The victim. He is telling Jacob how wrong he is, and how much he would have done for them if only Jacob would have let him. He makes it all sound so good. So wise. But it's a massive load of crap.

Whenever you have taken even the smallest steps into new life and freedom, control will come in with the crap. And that load of crap will be tied up with a pretty bow. It will look nice. It will sound wise. It will seem like the smarter choice. It will look so good you'll wonder why you didn't see it before! So we have to be able to identify the crap—even when its appearance seems appealing. In the experience of stepping out of my own controlling situation, that ministry leader told me that I would never be hired in ministry again if I didn't return to him. Then he tried to get somebody else to convince me that things would be different. Both attempts were prettied-up loads of crap, but they were both appealing reasons to return to my old position. The thought of never working in ministry again frightened me. I had to put working in his ministry on my resume because it's all that I had, but what if he just gave me a bad reference wherever I applied? Did he really have this much control over me? If I went back, I wouldn't have to find out. And maybe things *would* be different. Could it be true? What if I'm just being young and naive? Should I return to my job if it can offer me a paycheck? I can get paid to do what I love—that sounds great! Right? Wrong! Thankfully, I said "no," and didn't give into control...because months later, what unfolded at that ministry was not good.

What is the load of crap that control is trying to sell you? It's probably some sort of lie that relates to one of the following:

If you don't have _____ in your life, you will not have:

- Comfort
- Safety
- Money
- Predictability
- Peace
- Status
- Friendships

The load of crap being presented to you most likely sounds appealing, and probably even a little bit true. How can we possibly gain the perspective to see through it? We begin to see that pretty little package for the load of crap that it is when we recognize it is speaking to our deepest desires for short-sighted *self-concern*. How can we possibly get the strength to break the cycle? Where can we find a source of strength that will give us the ability to say "no" to that load of crap that control is trying to sell us? This is particularly tough to do the older we get—our brains become used to routines, and sometimes even enjoy those routines even if they're destructive. There must be a way out...but how?

LOOKING BEYOND OURSELVES

Jacob offers some great help for us to look beyond our controlling situation, especially when the options being presented make it enticing to stay where we are. Whenever you try to step into freedom, the manipulation of control is right around the corner attempting to sell you a false bag of goods. We must not succumb, we must press on. But to press on, we must hold on to the promise of a greater power, a promise of greater worth and substance than the alternative—the promise of manipulation and coercion and control. Jacob knew this. Jacob was not only clinging to the instruction of God to move on (Genesis 31:12-13), but he was able to confront Laban face to face by appealing to a higher promise, a higher call that had been given to him by God. Jacob was no longer consumed with short-sighted self-concern. Instead, he courageously confronted Laban because he was finally looking beyond himself.

> "These twenty years I have been in your house; I served you fourteen years for your two daughters and six years for your flock,

and you changed my wages ten times. *If the God of my father, the God of Abraham, and the fear of Isaac, had not been for me,* surely now you would have sent me away empty-handed. God has seen my affliction and the toil of my hands, so He rendered judgment last night."[19]

Jacob was clinging to the greater promise that God was for him! The same God who was for his grandfather Abraham and his father Isaac was for him. Twenty years before, God had spoken to Jacob in a dream and he had not forgotten God's promise that he would one day return. When you *experience* God you will be acquainted with the *promises* of God that empower you to step into the *potential* he designed you for.

As a senior in high school I was in a difficult position. I had no idea what I was going to do with my life. By the time my older brother was a sophomore he had the next thirty years of his life planned out. So as a senior, having absolutely *no plan* was not ideal. In January of my senior year I tried "seeking God"—and it worked! God spoke to me in these words from the apostle Paul, "But you, be sober in all things, endure hardship, do the work of an *evangelist*,

---

19 Genesis 31:41-42

fulfill your *ministry*."[20] In that verse I felt God tell me that he was calling me to a ministry of evangelizing to people who either wanted nothing to do with Jesus or had walked away from church. The ministry to which he was calling me was to one day start a church that reached people who nobody else was reaching.

Fast forward a few years. I'm the middle of the bad ministry situation that I've been writing about, and the pastor is playing the game of either trying to destroy my reputation or convince me to return. What gave me the strength and the confidence to say "no"—especially when it seemed at the time that my career and my future was in hands? I made a choice to live in the reality of the promise. God promised me my senior year of High School that he had a ministry for me, and it would one day come to fruition in planting a church.

I had no evidence of this promise other than what I believed God had said to me. I trusted in his promise over the lie that was attempting to control me. Time and again, when I have been at a crossroads or been tempted to make a poor decision, I am reminded of the promise God has over my life. This promise allows me to step out of my own control. This promise allows me to move beyond seeing things through my own self-concerned perspective, and instead, to live in the perspective of God's concern for the

---

20 2 Timothy 4:5

world around me. Do not allow anyone to gain control over the promise that God has over your life.

PROMISES, PROMISES, PROMISES

I cannot tell you what specific promises God has spoken over your life. In order for you to find that, you must spend time with him and listen for the voice of his Holy Spirit. Seek him and seek after who he created you, designed you, and wired you to be. Here are three concepts to consider when seeking God's promises over your life:

First, just because God promised you something that doesn't mean the path to get to that place will be easy. God will begin to shape your character for a greater purpose. This often requires discovering things about ourselves that we do not like. He will also shape us through perseverance, endurance, or persecution. Sometimes, outside of our control, life just gets dark, a tragedy strikes, and the ensuing trial doesn't appear to line up with the promise. These difficult times are a part of God's process. Struggles along your journey are to be expected. Mine and Kim's journey to plant a church has not always been easy—even though we can see it is headed in the direction of our experience with God, God's promise, and God's potential for us. Potential is good, but having potential to become one thing is also the potential to become something else, a distraction from God's calling. The road to fulfilling your potential in Christ can be difficult even when it's rooted in his promises. In those times of difficulty, we must seek to experience him more, learn to trust him more, and he will bring us peace.

Secondly, the pursuit of God's promise in your life will require a risk. The risk will demonstrate that you are now trusting God over trusting that which had control over you. Consider this: your demonstration of trust is not some kind of proof to God. He knows your ability. He's aware of your potential. He is intimate with your level of fatih. Your demonstration of trust is for—you. When you take the risk and trust in God's providence and his promise, you discover for yourself just how much you trust him! You are trusting the uncertainty of freedom over the illusion of certainty that is offered when you are under someone else's control.

Thirdly, while I may not know God's specific promises to you, there are some general promises from God that he speaks over your life. These are promises you can *always* cling to, specifically once you have lost your life and found it in Jesus.

God will never leave you.

When God is for us no one can stand against us.

God works all things out for the good of those who love him.

God desires for you to have abundant life.

You are a *new* creation in Christ.

This is just a short list of promises from God, but he holds the greater power to make these promises that we can cling to. When we *experience* God, we can cling to these *promises* as we step into the space that is our *potential.* The false promise, the manipulative lie of control is looking for you. The only way to step out of that cycle is by calling upon a greater power. That greater power is the promise from God that calls you into your potential! Get to know the promises of God by pursuing an experiential relationship with him. God's promise over your life is not just for you, it's also for the benefit of others (as we will discover later with Jacob). The promise of your potential brings you into a perspective of concern that is beyond self-concern and is *for* the good of others!

God's promises lead to God's potential which leads to God's concern.

God's concern is always for the good of others!

FOUR

Wrestling

I know very little about wrestling. When I was in sixth grade they only allowed seventh and eighth graders to be on the wrestling team. So I decided, along with one of my friends, to try to be a manager on the wrestling team. This was not a good experience for me. The wrestling room was hot, smelly, and kind of gross, and the overall environment was just not my vibe. I also have a friend who goes by the name of "Mr. Brickster" who is now a professional wrestler, and I've attended some of his matches. Literally, those two things are the extent of my knowledge of wrestling.

While I have never physically wrestled, It would be appropriate to say that I have mentally wrestled with concepts, ideas, thoughts, and yes, even in my faith. To wrestle is to "struggle with a difficulty or problem." In the time between leaving the house of Laban and returning to his homeland to confront his situation with Esau, Jacob engages in a wrestling match with God. This is a necessary moment in Jacob's life, and in ours as well. We must all come to a place in our lives where we wrestle with the concept and idea of God. I have outlined this chapter like a ride on a bus or a subway. We have a destination, a place we want to go, but we have to make four stops before we get there:

First Stop: Look at Jacob's wrestling match and what it means for us.

Second Stop: Address my more "Conservative Fundamentalist Faith" friends.[21]

Third Stop: Address my more "Deconstructionist Liberal Faith" friends.

Fourth Stop: Tie all of the stops together and create a path forward for each of us.

Let's step into the ring!

FIRST STOP

Jacob's journey has led him away from his life with Laban and he is now on his way to meet Esau. Jacob sends messengers ahead to inform Esau of his coming, and they return to Jacob with the message that Esau is on his way to meet

---

21 In using the terms "conservative" and "liberal," I'm speaking strictly within the realm of faith. I'm NOT speaking politically.

Jacob—with four hundred men. Jacob becomes afraid. Four hundred men? Is Esau coming to fight? So Jacob tries to ease the tension by sending a generous present to Esau. He divides his people, flocks and herds into two groups. Then he sent his wives and children ahead, and he spent the night alone. You can feel the tension of the unpredictability of freedom in this moment. That night, Jacob's solitude is interrupted, as he engages in a seemingly random and rather odd wrestling match with God.

(Then Jacob was left alone, and a man wrestled with him until daybreak. When he saw that he had not prevailed against him, he touched the socket of his thigh; so the socket of Jacob's thigh was dislocated while he wrestled with him.)

God: "Let me go, for the dawn is breaking."

Jacob: "I will not let you go unless you bless me."

God: "What is your name?

Jacob: "Jacob"

God: "Your name shall no longer be Jacob, but Israel; for you have striven with God and with men and have prevailed."

45

Jacob: "Please tell me your name."

God: "Why is it that you ask my name?"

(And he blessed him there. So Jacob named the place Peniel)

Jacob: "I have seen God face to face, yet my life has been preserved."

(Now the sun rose upon him just as he crossed over Penuel, and he was limping on his thigh.)[22]

Honestly, this is a bit of a strange story. It begins by stating that a man wrestled with Jacob, and then it turns out the man is God. After Jacob seemingly wins the match, God dislocates Jacob's thigh, and then it appears as if Jacob forces God to bless him. What exactly is happening here? In principle, I understand the importance of wrestling with the concept of God—but physically wrestling with God? I need to do some research on this one...BRB[23] (remember using this abbreviation on AIM back in the day?).

Okay...I'm back. One fun fact is that it turns out Jacob is ninety-seven years old at this point. Ninety-seven and in

---

22 Genesis 32:24-31
23 "Be right back."

a wrestling match? I think this takes the story to another level of outlandishness. One of my favorite explanations comes from John Goldingay, an Old Testament scholar. I considered giving you a summary, but I decided to just give you his own words. This explanation is a little long, but you need to read it as it brings great clarity.

So why is God wrestling with Jacob? God has been doing that all of Jacob's life, trying to turn Jacob into the man God wants him to be but failing. Here is God trying again but succeeding only by cheating, which means the victory is hollow. Perhaps one reason God appears just as a man is that this makes it a fair fight. If God overwhelms us simply through having superior fire power, it is not much use as a victory. God has to "win us," as we say. We have to want to yield to God's purpose and God's vision for us if the change in us is to be authentic. But Jacob does not want to yield and never does.

Yet God does bless him and gives him a new name that epitomizes his nature. As is often the case, the comment about the names has some subtleties about it. It links Jacob's new name with the fact that he is the great fighter. And yes indeed, Jacob is a person who keeps fighting with God in order to stay the man he is. In the end God lets him do that because God cannot force people to change. God can only make them limp. Yet a neophyte Hebraist would know that "Isra-el" does not actually mean "he fights/persists/exerts himself with God." It is a statement of which God is the subject—as God was the initiator of the fight in the story. If anything, "Isra-el" would mean "God fights/persists/exerts himself." God strives to get a person like Jacob to become the kind of person he could be and should be and that God wants him to be, and keeps at it in the struggle with Jacob.[24]

Thank you for hanging in there. I know that is a lot, especially if you're not familiar with this whole faith thing. If you want further research behind Jacob wrestling with God, go buy a commentary, and enjoy researching! I want to highlight a particular theme from Goldingay's perspective: God has been wrestling with Jacob all of his life. This situation demonstrates the heart of God, that he is not going to force us into anything, he will even condescend to our level if it means he can change our hearts to move beyond *self-concern*, and into *his greater concern* for humanity. God persists. He *never* gives up on you.

The Almighty God is inviting you into a wrestling match with him (not physically). In this wrestling match you will discover who God is, and that he wants you to

---

24 John Goldingay, *Genesis for Everyone*, p.118.

discover who he has created you and called you to be. This is an open invitation from God, and the door never closes. He is not afraid of our questions, objections, and doubts. He just desires for us to step into that wrestling match, that challenging conversation with him. The love of God is such that he will not force anything on you, but that he will still desire what is best for you. Will you step into the ring?

SECOND STOP

I have had at least one foot in the faith community for as long as I can remember. My parents raised me in church until about seventh grade. At one point, my family was hurt by the church so we didn't go for a number of years. Later, in High School, I worked at a Christian Camp, and during my senior year I felt called to ministry. Since that calling, for almost a decade of my life, I have either been working in a ministry setting or heavily involved, and now I'm a church planter. When you're as involved as I am in the faith community, you encounter some interesting people.

The church as a whole is generally an amazing group of people. A church can be a wonderful support system for faith, encouragement, and personal growth. But like any movement the church also has its share of bad apples. One group of bad apples is an overly conservative fundamental group. This group does not have an official denomination or name, but they exist in every church and ministry. These people know better than everyone else, and they can give you great clarity on what everyone else is doing "wrong" or how everyone else is "living in sin." If we are not careful we can all become one of these people. I will admit that for a season of my life I *was* one of these people. Being that I was one of these people, here is what I can confidently say about them: This group of people has avoided wrestling with God.

During this section of the book, if you feel a tension rising and you are tempted to throw this book (or your kindle) across the room, chances are you are one of these overly conservative people. You are more concerned about protecting your beliefs that make you feel superior to others than actually wrestling with knowing who God is. If you find yourself frequently saying or thinking one of the following things, you may be one of these people...or on the verge of becoming one of these people.

- "I'm not gossiping about this person, I'm just warning you about them."
- "God says it, that settles it."
  This statement can be true, but oftentimes what it's communicating is: "I don't want to listen to other people's perspective or interpretation of Scripture."
- "Christians should only listen to Christian music."
- "All Christians should vote for _____ party. The United States is God's country and we must protect it."

Really? When did the United States become a theocracy?

- "I'm not judging you, I'm just speaking the truth."

- Whenever the government does something you don't like you scream "persecution"

- Whenever someone puts something on social media that you disagree with you think it is your job to publicly correct them with the "obvious" answer.

- You cringe or treat someone as inferior whenever someone asks a question that you assume has a clear answer.

- "Never question what the pastor says. God placed him there."
  I cannot overstate how dangerous this statement or mindset can be. Pastoral authority has its place, pastoral autonomy does not, and can lead to an abuse of power.

Not all of the above statements are direct correlations of overly conversative mindsets, but generally the above statements fall into that camp. Are you frustrated with me? Are you thinking of arguments of how you would correct me and totally destroy me in an argument? Congratulations! You are officially a part of this group. What's funny to me is that Jesus really opposed this group in his time. The

Pharisees and Sadducees had "all" of the right answers. Or at least they thought they did. What is interesting to me is that when someone steps into this legalistic realm, others will say of them, "Oh, they're just a little extreme." But if someone steps into a more liberal faith perspective they are quickly labeled "a heretic." Something to think about....

Why do I contend that this group does not wrestle with God? Two reasons. First, people in this group only listen to certain pastors and leaders and then classify other thoughts as "dangerous." If you have an inability to wrestle with other ideas and concepts, chances are you have not wrestled with God who transcends *all* ideas and concepts. Instead of having your own personal wrestling with God you have decided to just take whatever information your pastor or leader offers you and that informs your faith. There is no wrestling in this process; it's just a process of filling your mind with information that protects your tribe, along with strengthening all of your own confirmation biases.

Secondly, remember how I said I was in this group for awhile? "Hello, my name is Scott and I'm a recovering conservative fundamentalist." When I was about nineteen years old I began to ask some questions. I was having a bit of an internal faith crisis, and I began to ask some questions. I realized two things:

1. Some questions are not welcome in this community.

2. Sometimes a question can be welcome if it's asked the "right way."

Just a word of warning. If you are ever in an environment where questions are not welcome—*get out!* That is a tell-tale sign of a cult. Or if you have to clarify your questions or ask them in a certain way, be careful. For example, at that time I was struggling with some statements in the Bible. I knew that if I admitted that I had questions about the Bible I would be met with condemnation, and maybe even be referred to as "lost" or "going down the wrong path." So to avoid this kind of branding, when asking questions I would say things like, "My friend is struggling with the Bible. Do you have any resources that I could give to him?" I felt like I had to hide my own questions because of the consequences of asking.

My experience was a confirmation to me that this group does not encourage true wrestling with God. If you are in this mindset, you must step out of it. One day in the future a good friend, a family member, or your child is going to ask you one of the following questions, and your response *could* determine how they handle their wrestling process.

- What does it mean to know God?
- Can God really set me free from my pain?
- Isn't it inhumane for God to flood the earth?

- Does the Old Testament support genocide?
- Do we really believe that David fought a giant?
- Why would a good God send people to Hell?
- Isn't the Bible's teaching on gender roles outdated?
- Wasn't the Bible just put together by humans? What makes it so special?
- Why doesn't God stop bad things from happening?
- Do we really believe that Jesus actually lived and actually died and actually came back from the dead? [25]

The above list is just a handful of questions that people will ask. How you respond to these questions could determine whether their next step is closer to God...or a step away from him. When people ask these questions a quick "Sunday School answer" will not help or survive in the age of information. The best way to help people with their questions is to listen, and listen some more. Then after you do that, listen some more. We must be quick to listen and slow to speak. We must allow people to wrestle with God. I would rather someone discover God through their questioning and digging instead of just receiving some

---

25 I'm by no means advocating that we need to change Christian doctrine/beliefs. I am advocating for a more gentle response to such questions.

apparently "right" answers from me about God that will only function as a band-aid until the question resurfaces again. I'm so confident in the presence and reality of who God is that I know that he will make himself real to them through their questioning .

But back to you. Are you in this camp? Are you a conservative fundamentalist? Have you never really wrestled with God? By no means do I want to destroy your faith. But asking some questions can actually lead to a stronger, more solidified faith. Reading and listening to some people who you strongly disagree with can actually draw you closer to God. My challenge would be to question everything. You will find that in your questioning God is present in the midst of the questioning. You won't be drawn away from faith but you will become a stronger person of faith. Step into other people's shoes and ask questions they are asking—just like Jesus stepped into our shoes by becoming human. When we read and listen to those we disagree with, it does three things:

1. Reading and listening allows us to learn where people are truly coming from (instead of just *assuming* that we know where they are coming from). News flash!! People's reasons for questioning faith today are not the same as they were ten years, twenty years, and thirty years ago.

2. Reading and listening strengthens our faith to actually consider why we believe what we believe. Be ready to learn that you have been wrong about some things.

3. Reading and listening ensures that God is the object of your pursuit every time and you will only grow closer to him. It was extremely liberating for me to step beyond the barrier of just knowing God through someone else's perspective by truly coming to know him personally.

If you are in this group. I ask that you pray about not being angry or frustrated by my words, but instead be challenged by them. I'm coming from a place of truly wanting more for you in your faith journey. When you go on this pursuit it will take you out of the prison of dogmatic, pharisaical self-concern, and you will be brought into the concern of God—which is the movement of God in the world. In Jesus' famous story of the prodigal son, once the rebellious son returns home, the older, obedient son is confused. He has followed all of the rules and says to his father:

> "Look! For so many years I have been serving you and I have never neglected a command of yours; and yet you have never given me a young goat, so that I might celebrate with my

friends; but when this son of yours came, who has devoured your wealth with prostitutes, you killed the fattened calf for him." [26]

The older son was in a prison. He had followed all of the rules, he did everything the right way. Why was the younger son, "the sinner" getting a party? The father informs the older son that all that he has is his. The older son, because of his self-concern, did not see the blessing of the father that was there all along. Do not allow a limited self-concern make you miss out on the blessing of God in your life. Step into the concern of God, the higher call, to love people, to talk with people, and discover with them who God is.

Will you step into the ring?

THIRD STOP

I used to hate musicals. Kim, on the other hand, loves musicals. About two and a half years into our marriage a movie called *The Greatest Showman* hit theaters. It was the first musical that I ever watched with Kim, and I really enjoyed it. My heart was being softened toward musicals. Less than a year later we went to see *Aladdin* At Shea's theater[27]. I also

---

26 Luke 15:29-30

27 Shea's is a magical theater in Buffalo for touring Broadway shows.

enjoyed *Aladdin*; my heart was truly being transformed. In November of 2018, we returned to Shea's to see a musical and it was one of the best productions that I had ever witnessed. *Hamilton!!!* If you have not seen *Hamilton*, stop reading this book right now. Get on Disney+ and watch *Hamilton* ASAP. The lyrics, the music, the character development... 🤯!!!

Hamilton is about Alexander Hamilton, one of the founding fathers of the United States of America. The majority of the play follows Hamiton's complicated relationship and political rivalry with Aaron Burr. Hamilton was a man of conviction. Burr was a true politician who would shape shift and change his perspective just to get ahead. At one point of the play, Hamilton says something to Burr that characterizes where I want to go with my deconstructionist friends. Hamilton says these powerful words to Burr, "If you stand for nothing, Burr, what will you fall for?"[28] We will unpack this statement more, because I'm convinced that many of my more liberal/deconstructionist-faith friends end up in a similar place with their faith that Aaron Burr does with his political persuasions. First, a few clarifying statements on the "church."

The Church is people. Therefore, the church has the capacity to hurt people. We cannot hide from abuse that has happened in the church. Sexual abuse, spiritual abuse,

---

28 "Aaron Burr, Sir," *Hamilton*, 2015.

authoritarian abuse. If you have been hurt by the church or abused by the church I do extend my apologies to you. Church hurt is real. There are levels of church hurt, and it's not easy to work through.

The Church is people. Therefore, the church has the capacity to be wrong. When you are given wrong information about life, faith, and the world, it can also be damaging. If you were given bad information by the church, again, I apologize. The perpetuation of this kind of misinformation can lead to very embarrassing conversations and naivety within the church.

The Church is people. Therefore the church has been and always will be imperfect. Just remember, you are also part of that imperfection. We must recognize that we are not perfect people, and our is not the most perfect generation. My generation has an obsession with overanalyzing all of the sins and wrongdoings of previous generations without taking into account that somebody could do the same thing to us in thirty, forty, or fifty years from now. We have a responsibility to do our best, but we will also get things wrong. Instead of spending all of our time criticizing the past, we would be better off spending our energy on building a better future.

I personally know a lot of people who are in this deconstructionist perspective when it comes to faith. I have read books and listened to podcasts that represent a deconstructionist perspective. It appears as if there is a push in the

West to redefine faith. Some of this is necessary. Much of the reason for the reform that we see in this movement comes from the above concerns, church hurt and abuse, misinformation and judgmentalism, and the overall state of the church's imperfection (often taking the form of self-righteous people who act as if they are perfect). These inconsistencies have caused people to ask questions.

On top of all of that, we live in the age of information. We have access to great thinkers and theologians from around the world. With all of these elements, it is *necessary* to deconstruct our faith, to get rid of the noise and the traditions and cultural additions and obfuscations, and consider just how God is speaking to the present circumstances of the modern world. Deconstruction *must* happen, but deconstruction *without reconstruction* is irresponsible.

The issue at hand is that deconstructionist thinkers have a tendency to deconstruct, and then never reconstruct. Once again, I want to state that I'm generally a fan of deconstructing. It keeps us on our toes. I have deconstructed many things in my faith journey. What my deconstructionists fail to see is that when they choose to live in a deconstruction quagmire and never reconstruct, they are being equally as intellectually lazy as the fundamentalists that they have rebelled against. When you only deconstruct, you are wrestling with God for a while and then just sitting on the mat. You must finish the wrestling match by reconstructing, then you can move forward. You have a responsibility to move beyond your self-concern and move forward to working for the good of others. If you don't finish the wrestling match you end up wallowing in self-concern because you don't have any convictions about responsibility. It's all based in, "I don't know." Here are my six reasons as to why I wish my deconstructionist friends would wrestle with God to a place of reconstruction.

1. Reconstructing brings us to a greater place of humility.

Deconstructing your faith or walking away from your faith usually comes from a point of rebellion, or rejection. Finding yourself at the point of rebellion can actually have some roots of humility—the humility to recognize that the religious fundamentalists do no not know everything, and they do not have an easy answer for everything. This is a journey of humility because you do not want to be filled with an arrogance that assumes you "know" every-thing. The problem is if you sit in your deconstruction for too long without any attempts at reconstruction you can also become arrogant in a deconstructionist perspective. You begin to assume that nobody is asking the questions you are asking, and that nobody has any type of resolution for the questions you are asking. You dismiss all perspec-tives unless they affirm your confirmation bias. When you begin to reconstruct you have to step back into a journey of humility. You must admit that maybe you were wrong about some things, and that possibly even people you thought were at one time wrong may actually be right. You may discover that some of the truths they presented were right, but delivered with a wrong attitude. Do not allow your deconstructionism to lead to arrogance.

We have to understand that we have the capacity to get "it" wrong. Your generation, my generation, whatever generation you are a part of (Boomer, Gen X, Millennial, Z, and the generations to come) is not a sinless generation. One definition of sin is to "miss the mark," and every generation will "miss the mark" in *some* way. We must have the humility to realize that we will sin. We must also have the humility to forgive other generations for their sin and celebrate their victories. We cannot define a generation strictly by their sin, by the marks they missed. You wouldn't want someone doing that to your generation, and certainly not to you personally. Have the humility to understand, forgive, and celebrate. "Grace" is the operative word here!

2. Reconstructing takes work.

All of us have been in a place of being lazy with our faith. When you sit in deconstructionism without ever asking questions—and re-asking questions—you become just as lazy as the fundamentalists that you walked away from. Reconstructing takes the work of once again wrestling with your faith, discovering truth, and finding conviction in it. And once you have begun to reconstruct, even more work is required because you begin to function from that place of conviction. Do you really want to live the rest of your life continually shape shifting in conversations and responding to every difficult topic with "I don't know"? Don't get me wrong, there is wisdom in not speaking on things of which you don't have all of the information. But there is also wisdom in saying things like, "I don't necessarily know the right thing to do, but based on what I do know, this is the wise thing to do." If deconstruction is a demolition job then reconstruction is picking up the rubble and doing the work to rebuild.

3. Reconstructing requires responsibility.

One of the questions we forgot to ask is, "What kind of foundation are we building for the next generation?" Sometimes I get concerned that deconstruction is building a culture of doubt for the next generation instead of a culture of faith. Doubt is a good thing, but it can also be dangerous if it leads to a continual suspicion of all things at all times. We must build a generation of faith. Faith in God and faith in others. When we lose faith in God and faith in other people, how can we as humanity work together to build a better future? Reconstructing requires us to be responsible for our actions because we are acting out of a place of conviction from a solidified faith. Acting from conviction means when we make the "right" choice we celebrate our victories. When we make the "wrong" choice we hold ourselves and one another accountable and grow together. If you just live in a place of deconstruction there is no reason to celebrate victories and there is no source of accountability for wrong actions, because everything is rooted in a place of "I don't know."

4. Reconstructing means surrendering moral high ground.

When you began to deconstruct, or when you walked away from faith, one of the things that probably frustrated you was the sense of moral superiority that religious fundamentalists subscribed to. Not only did they impose moral authority, but they were also major hypocrites, right? I would agree with you on both of those points. But while I agree with you, here is the issue I have run into: Many of my more liberal deconstructionist friends love to ask questions, but oftentimes they become very frazzled if your answer does not align with their answer. The pendulum has actually shifted and you didn't even notice it. Deconstructionists tend to assume that they have read a book, listened to a podcast, or obtained some information that *nobody* else has access to, and then they have a tendency to get frustrated with people who don't adopt their perspective.

Often when I'm talking with my deconstructionist friends, I begin to feel the same way as when I'm talking with my overly conservative fundamentlist friends. I get a feeling of condemnation for not "seeing" or not "adopting" their perspective. Just like the fundamentalists, they are truly not okay with a different perspective. If you are a deconstructionist, ask yourself this question, "Have I become just like the people that I rebelled against?" When you begin to reconstruct it requires you to surrender your moral high ground. You have to be willing to say, "I might be wrong about _____." When you find an answer, it's okay to live in a conviction of, "I believe _____ to be right." Conviction allows your life to move in a direction. Having a conviction that the other way is wrong is only an opinion until it is firmly rooted in something.

5. Reconstructing requires a blueprint.

If you tore down a house that was structurally unsound, would you begin rebuilding without a blueprint? If you don't know what you are building, you risk building something as structurally unsound as the last house, or even worse! When we wrestle with God and wrestle with our faith, we have to decide what it is we are wrestling with. Are you struggling with belief in God? There is a lot of work to be done. A foundation to be torn up. This is not the time to begin reconstruction. Are you struggling with how God has been presented or portrayed by judgemental Christians. Are you struggling with how truths have been conveyed by Christian teachers? Are you struggling with how love has been displayed by people in your church?

These are great things to wrestle with. These are things that drive us to a point of deconstruction. "Something is wrong here. Something has to change." Do we rip out walls or do we fire up the bulldozer?

But reconstructing takes an examination. We doubt because something seems amiss with the way things are. We say "I don't know" because things are no longer clear. But in the same way Jacob wrestled, we cling to God. We hold on tight. I saw the dream. He spoke to me. He holds the answer. "I don't know, but God *does*." Search his Word to find truth. Compare your reasons for doubt with what the Bible tells us is right and good. And there you will find conviction. And with conviction comes direction. And direction becomes your blueprint for reconstruction.

6. Reconstructing moves you beyond self-concern.

Living in deconstruction for too long moves us into a place of self-concern. We are more concerned with feeling comfortable about our convictions. The goal is not that we should always be uncomfortable about our convictions, but we should feel challenged by them. When everything is "I don't know," you're not receiving your challenge, your call, your convictions from a higher power, but instead you're personally defining all of those things based on your preference in the moment. That is the most self-concerned thing that you could possibly do because it's all about *you* attempting to build a life that is best for *you*. Instead, *the goal should be for us to build a life that is best for others.* The one who best demonstrated how to live a life that is *others* focused was Jesus. Jesus lived from a place of challenge, call, and conviction. If Jesus is the archetypal figure for humanity, then shouldn't we desire to function as he did?

Typically I hear people say things like, "I just want to love people." Great! So do I! We all do (I hope). But how can you define love if there is not a source of love? When we deconstruct so far from Jesus, who, then, is defining love? Jesus *is* love. Humans can still experience a level of love without Christ, but Christ is the most pure expression and example of love. Therefore, reconstructing our faith around him gets us to a place of true love, because he is love.

Lastly, on this point we must consider that at times deconstruction is not a true wrestling with God. Your deconstruction may have begun with wrestling with God, but after some time, deconstruction can develop into:

- Wrestling with people who claim to represent God.
- Wrestling with a specific doctrine of Christianity.
- Wrestling with some of your own internal questions, etc.

Are you truly wrestling with God? I would contend that most deconstructionists have not stepped into the ring with God for a while. This is rooted in the same self-concern as religious fundamentalists. On the intimidating side, to step into the ring with God means you may find some things that you don't like or don't agree with. On the encouraging side, to step into the ring with God means that you grow closer to your purpose of working for the good because you have come to better know the *one* who is good. Who are you wrestling with? Move beyond the self-concern of your insulated world. Wrestle with God and begin to see the greater concern and conviction that he has for your life.

Once you have wrestled with God you can stand for something!

Which brings us back to our original question from Hamilton to Burr. Hamilton's question is a critical one for deconstructionists:

"If you stand for nothing, what will you fall for?"

FOURTH STOP

We are approaching our fourth and final stop in our wrestling with God. In light of our three previous stops, it seems appropriate to draw out one major theme. The theme is "empowerment." When you wrestle with God you are empowered to step into the future God has for you. Jacob is renamed "Israel" (Genesis 32:28) which means "God prevails." When you wrestle with God you will discover the prevailing will of God over your life, but you will also find he desires to have his prevailing will *at work in your life,* and *for your life!* With this new name, with this new identity, with this empowerment from God, Jacob can now face Esau.

Once you have wrestled with God and discover his prevailing will *over your life,* and *for* your life, you will see that you can face anything. You can face the very thing that has been keeping you from stepping into your future because God is on your side. Jacob became Israel. Israel became God's chosen people, and when they got their role right they brought hope to the world. Wrestling with God empowered Jacob to face his greatest fear, but it also shaped him into a new person who looked beyond his own self-concern. Jacob's family line, through his son Judah, became the catalyst of concern for all of humanity in Jesus.

Wrestle with God! Wrestling with God will allow you to discover things about yourself that you never knew were true. When you wrestle with God, facing the Esau of your life won't be so difficult. God is a much higher authority than the Esau you must face. Jacob was able to stand confidently and move forward into the unknown once he had wrestled with God.

Wrestle with God.

Wrestling with God will allow God to shape your identity just as he did with Jacob.

When God is at the core of your identity...

You can face the unknown.

You can move forward into a greater concern.

Wrestle with God and he will *break* your will so that you can step *into* his will.

FIVE

Get Over Yourself

As you move forward, journeying into the unknown of your greater concern for the world, you will face something intimidating: You will find yourself in conversations you feel unqualified to be in. When Kim and I stepped into planting a church we had to have conversations with people who had more life experience than us, were much smarter, and asked questions we were not ready to answer. I proceeded with the assumption that some people would immediately disapprove of our decision, and we did, in fact, receive some pushback:

"You're too young to start a church."

"Buffalo doesn't need another church."

"Your church won't be different than any other church."

"You won't be able to raise enough money."

"People won't follow someone like you."

Pushbacks are to be expected. The crazy thing was, sometimes I would enter a conversation with someone about whom I made the assumption they would be against what we were doing, but they were actually totally *for* it. They were completely encouraging. Shame on me for assuming the worst! I began to realize something I already knew to be true, but had forgotten: "People are not thinking about me and criticizing me as much I think that they are."

The same is true for you. People are not thinking about you nearly as much as you think they are. I guarantee this. The truth is, nobody thinks about you as much as *you* think about you. And the negative things that you assume people are thinking about you are typically not true. People have enough of their own problems. They have their own social media platforms to scroll through and play the comparison game with. They're too busy wondering what people think of them. Sorry to break it to you—but you are not at the center of as many people's thoughts as you may think.

REUNITED

Jacob has been assuming that Esau has been thinking about nothing but getting back at him ever since Jacob left. Jacob sent messengers to Esau. The messengers return and inform Jacob that Esau is coming with four hundred men (Genesis 32:7). Jacob assumes that he is bringing four hundred men to intimidate him, or worse. While waiting for Esau, Jacob wrestles with God, and through that event, Jacob is given a newfound confidence—but there is still some fear on his part.

Then Jacob lifted his eyes and looked, and behold, Esau was coming, and four hundred men with him. So he divided the children among Leah and Rachel and the two maids. He put the maids and their children in front, and Leah and her children next, and Rachel and Joseph last. But he himself passed on ahead of them and bowed down to the ground seven times, until he came near to his brother.[29]

Jacob breaks up his family in order to protect them. He begins bowing out of reverence for his brother. It has been over twenty years, and Jacob is assuming that Esau has been holding a grudge this entire time. What if Esau is still angry about the whole birthright and blessing thing? That would be justifiable, right?

Esau is stronger.

Esau could hurt Jacob.

Esau could kill Jacob.

Was it worth it to leave Laban for this?

How might you respond if you were Esau? I know people who haven't talked with loved ones for years over a single disagreement. Many of us have witnessed this level of tension in the family, when everyone comes together for a happy occasion and an estranged family member arrives.

---

29 Genesis 33:1-3

There is an aggression bubbling beneath the surface, and everyone is left wondering when somebody is going to snap. Family drama is real. And this is the climax of the Jacob and Esau family drama. What is going to happen?

> Then Esau ran to meet him and embraced him, and fell on his neck and kissed him, and they wept.[30]

Anti-climatic and a beautiful response all at the same time. Just as Jacob had moved on with his life, Esau had moved on with his. Jacob had grown, changed, and evolved, and so has Esau. Esau was just happy to be with his brother once again. Esau was not thinking about Jacob as much as Jacob thought he was. They were both adults with successes and families. Esau realized something that many of us need to realize. You cannot sit around for twenty years wishing things would have gone differently. Eventually you have to find a new sense of responsibility and move forward. Esau even calls Jacob out for bringing so many things with him.

> **Esau:** "What do you mean by all this company which I have met?"

> **Jacob:** "To find favor in the sight of my lord."

---

30 Genesis 33:4

Esau: "I have plenty, my brother; let what you have be your own." [31]

Forgiveness is given and brothers are reunited. Esau is so elated that he even offers to journey with Jacob (Genesis 33:12). And even though Jacob denies the offer, that doesn't take away the power of forgiveness and the power of moving forward.

Get over yourself. You can face your past. You can face the tension. Once you have wrestled with God and discovered who he says you are you can step into the places he has called you.

YOUR PARALYZING PAST

I'm not a psychologist. I'm not a therapist. I'm not going to pretend to be one. Some pastors attempt to be both. Some pastors claim that neither are necessary. I believe that both of these approaches lack wisdom. While I'm neither a psychologist nor a therapist, there is a concept from both Jacob and Esau that we must wrestle with. Since I'm not a psychologist or therapist, I won't dive into specifics on how to deal with these two things—that's above my paygrade—but I do want to speak from a general perspective because this is helpful for us in moving beyond self-concern.

---

31 Genesis 33:8-9

If we journey back to Jacob and Esau's upbringing, they had very different pasts. Jacob's life was sent on an unfortunate trajectory because of bad decisions he was responsible for. Esau's life was sent on an unfortunate trajectory because he was a victim of someone else's bad decisions and manipulation. We all at one point in our lives have been in one of these categories, or maybe even both:

1. Your future has been affected by bad decisions that you are responsible for.

2. Your future has been affected by bad things that happened to you.

3. Both.

As a result:

- How can we possibly move forward?
- What if you have done something so reprehensible that it cannot be forgiven?
- What if your decisions affect how people view you?
- What if something has happened to you that is so paralyzing that you cannot move forward? *We will explore this question further in Chapter Eight.*
- What if what happened to you years ago affects how you relate to others today?

The process or the necessary steps you may need to undergo to work through some of these questions are typically best found in prayer and professional counseling. For me to try and offer "three easy steps" would be foolish for two reasons: First, remember, I'm not a counselor or a therapist. Second, there is not a one-size-fits-all solution for these types of questions. There is, however, an inevitable truth about life that at some point in time your past will come back and confront you in some way, and in those moments you have to determine how you will respond. What I can speak confidently on, based on Jacob and Esau, coupled with my story and other people's stories, is the power of forgiveness.

FORGIVENESS IS MORE THAN SAYING "SORRY"

For anyone who is a fan of early 2000's romantic comedies starring Ryan Reynolds, you may recognize the above subtitle as the lyrics from the song by Anna Farris' character in the movie *Just Friends*. The statement is true. Forgiveness is not just saying "sorry" and moving on. Forgiveness requires truly being set free from what someone did to you and moving on. Forgiveness is a required part of life. Without forgiveness, we can become fully subjected to our past. When we choose not to forgive we place a cap on our capacity to grow, along with placing a cap on another person's capacity to grow.

After everything Jacob did to Esau, Esau chose to forgive Jacob. If we had to read into the story, we can most likely assume that there were times when Esau probably bullied Jacob in childhood, therefore, Jacob also had to forgive Esau. Forgiveness propelled each of them to step into the future God had for them. Forgiveness is saying, "I'm not going to live in the past or be controlled by the past, but instead, I'm moving into the future."

Forgiveness is one of the central themes that make the way of Jesus so compelling. Have you ever been in a position where you are convinced that you have done nothing wrong, and therefore, you will not extend an apology? Let's be honest, most of us have been there before. "I didn't do anything wrong, why should *I* apologize?" Even if you're still unsure about the whole following Jesus thing, think about this.

Jesus did nothing wrong.

Yet he willingly gave his life.

He was beaten.

Mocked.

Crucified on a cross.

Before he died on that cross, Jesus looked at those who were mocking him. Instead of saying "I didn't do anything wrong. I'm not going to forgive them," Jesus rises above the circumstance. Jesus, who from a human standard is a victim of injustice and abuse, says these very powerful words, "Father, forgive them; for they do not know what they are doing."[32]

---

32 Luke 23:34

Stop.

Think of the person you are choosing to not forgive.

Breathe.

Put this book down.

Sit on that thought for a while.

...

Thanks for coming back. Jesus extends that forgiveness to each and every one of us. Even when we have done things that we know are wrong, He still extends forgiveness to us. His forgiveness gives us a clean slate and a new label, just like Jacob who had a new name! His forgiveness offers us a new reality. When Jesus went to the cross to be a sacrifice for humanity, he was doing that so we as humans could have a new future. Forgiveness is the way forward into the future. Just as we have been forgiven of the evil that we have done, we have been called to extend that forgiveness toward others. This is the way of progress, this is the way of the future.

> "For if you forgive others for their transgressions, your heavenly Father will also forgive you. But if you do not forgive others, then your Father will not forgive your transgressions."[33]

"Be kind and compassionate to one another, forgiving each other, just as in Christ God forgave you."

---

33 Matthew 6:14-15

Forgive as you have been forgiven! Let's step into the story of forgiveness that we were called to. Forgiveness is never easy, but it's always worth it. Let's move forward in building a future of forgiveness!

NASTY NARCISSISM

There is one last thing we must address in this section of Jacob's journey that we kind of breezed over. Within each of these stories there are major themes and minor themes. The major theme of the reconciliation between Jacob and Esau is clearly the power of forgiveness. One of the minor themes is *Narcissism*. The word narcissism is thrown around a lot today. It will be helpful for us to gain a clear definition. Dictionary.com defines narcissism as "inordinate fascination with oneself; excessive self-love; vanity."[34] That will be an appropriate functioning definition for our purposes.

Jacob, by all means, struggled with narcissism. When somebody is so self-obsessed regarding what someone else thinks of them, then narcissism is definitely involved. Vanity at it's finest is played out. There are levels of narcissism, and this is an issue that must be discussed. The root of self-concern is narcissism. When you're functioning from self-concern you're functioning from a perspective that the world is revolving around you; you have become fascinated with *self.*

---

34 https://www.dictionary.com/browse/narcissism

The way the message of Christianity has been communicated in our modern Western society in some ways propagates a narcissistic view of the world. Whether you were raised with a Christian worldview or not, you were probably in some way affected by this worldview. To be clear, I don't think that a truly Christian worldview propagates narcissism, but I do believe that the way in which modern western culture has twisted the Christian message does propagate narcissism.

I was raised in church, and attended a Christian youth camp multiple times in my youth. The first time that I can recall the Christian message really resonating with me was when I was about ten years old. After this, I heard this message over and over and over again. Each time I heard the message I literally had the hell scared out of me. Who wouldn't want to give their life to Jesus if the alternative means burning in hell for all of eternity? Pretty convincing argument if you ask me. When we as humans have such a great temptation for self-concern and self-preservation, we want to avoid pain at any costs.

Evangelicals typically start the message by quoting Paul: "For all have sinned and fall short of the glory of God."[35] To this day I believe that statement to be true, but it's not the best starting point. Is the fact that you are a sinner the first thing that God wants you to know about yourself?

---

35 Romans 3:23

That's debatable.

It all depends on where you go from there. (More on this in Chapter Nine.)

Where many evangelicals typically go from there is unwrapping a series of other verses which basically explain that you better give your life to Jesus so that you can go to Heaven. A picture is painted where the goal of Christianity is to go to Heaven, and you feel like because of your sin God would prefer you just go to hell, but he sent his son to die for you because he had to. You pray a prayer in which you say "all of the right words" so that you can go to Heaven. This is a guilt-based faith that can subtly lead to narcissism.

How does this lead to narcissism? In taking the gospel to focus on you as a sinner and God being angry with you creates a narrative that is very self-centered. You are constantly wondering things like.

- "Did I make God mad today?"
- "I prayed the prayer, but I sinned. Will I still be accepted into Heaven?"
- "I was very well behaved today. Did God notice? Will others see how righteous I am?"
- "I forgot to read my Bible for the past three days. Does that mean I won't make it to Heaven?"
- "I prayed the prayer a long time ago. Did I fully understand? Should I pray it again?"
- "I just hope I don't go to hell."

The questions are endless, and none of them have to do with God and his purpose for the world, but they all have to do with you. All of these questions and statements are rooted in self-concern. Don't worry, I've been there before. This version of faith is all about keeping God happy and making sure people notice your works based on righteousness which means you will go to the good place when you die. Even if you didn't grow up with faith, you have been affected by this. I bet that you have felt this way about God before, and I am sure you have met people who act this way.

The view of God that I'm describing has led to a group of people in the church who have a horrible self-esteem. Why? Because in God's view they are nothing but a sinner, and if they make one wrong decision it might indicate that they didn't take the salvation prayer seriously. People either cling to this version of Christianity and go through life always worried about what God thinks about them—and what other people think about them—or they get exhausted by this version of faith and walk away. Let's face it, after a while narcissism and self-concern become exhausting. The sad thing is that those who walk away end up indulging in other forms of narcissism from a self-centered worldview that says, "I'm my own boss now." It's all a horrible cycle, and it could have been prevented if we had been given a more accurate picture of who God is.

Ready for another Jim Carrey reference? In 2003, Jim Carrey starred in a movie called *Bruce Almighty*. Bruce is a weather man in the greatest city in the world: BUFFALO, NY! He is convinced that God is out to get him. Bruce's perspective of God leads Bruce to say the following to his girlfriend: "God is a mean kid sitting on an anthill with a magnifying glass, and I'm the ant. He could fix my life in five minutes if He wanted to, but He'd rather burn off my feelers and watch me squirm."[36] What a tragic, yet accurate, description of how so many people feel about God. We have a picture of a God who only wants you to think about yourself and how displeased with you he is. And on your good days, how happy he is with you! This is all one big invitation to narcissism and self-concern. This is an invitation into a lifestyle where people are scared to take responsibility, to take risks, and to pursue meaningful endeavours because, "What if it's not in God's will for my life?"

God doesn't want us living in this type of confusion. God doesn't want us living as a people who are bogged down in self-concern. The invitation to follow Jesus is far greater than that. At the core of the Christianity that many of us grew up with, Jesus saved you for your sake. *What if Jesus didn't save you merely for your own sake? What if he saved you for the sake of others?* Don't misread what I'm saying, there are great personal benefits to following Jesus:

---

36   https://www.moviequotes.com/s-movie/bruce-almighty/

- Grace
- Mercy
- Forgiveness
- Freedom
- Abundant Life
- Eternal Life

We could go on forever with the personal benefits. There are great personal benefits when we step into a relationship with Jesus. *But, what if those things happened to you and through you not just for you, but for someone else? What if the saving work of Jesus was to give you confidence to step into the world, as opposed to isolating away from the world?* When we begin to follow Jesus, we step into a life that is no longer "me first," but it's a life that is "others first." The life of Jesus was always others first, so our lives should be the same.

We don't have to fret about where we stand with God. Once you have chosen to follow Jesus he is clear that you cannot be snatched out of his hand (John 10:28). The central call from Jesus is to love God and love others (Matthew 22:37-39). This is a call to a greater concern, and it's not to be taken lightly. We take this call seriously. We don't take this call seriously because he may get mad at us and smite us if we do the wrong thing. We take the call seriously because when we love him we follow his ways (John 14:15). This is a call *from* love and *for* love. The way of Jesus is for others, so that others may find the freedom that is found in Jesus alone (John 8:32). If you have been bogged down by the narcissistic Christianity of your youth, let Christ set you free. Step out of your own self-concern and into the concern of others. Live a life where you are willing to lay down your life for the good of others (John 15:13).

A NEW NAME

As I'm writing this chapter I just returned from a little drive that I took to Rochester, NY. Rochester is a little over an hour away from Buffalo, and I felt last night that the Holy Spirit was saying that I needed to go to Rochester to visit my brother-in-law John at work. John called me last night. He and his family are going through a difficult situation. He asked for prayer and I could tell he was burned out from the weight of the situation. This is one of those situations with no easy way out, and it must be dealt with. Some of this situation has affected Kim and I as well, along with other family members. It has been going on for almost a year and has no end in sight. I'm not going to go into the details of what is happening, but it's heavy, it's dark, and it's real. You have probably been in a similar place with your family before. The suffering of life is inevitable.

I woke up this morning with a number of tasks to accomplish, yet I had this feeling that I should drop those tasks, drive to Rochester, and bring John a Nitro Brew Coffee from Starbucks. I love seeing John, but driving two hours round-trip just to deliver a coffee did not sound appealing, especially in my Chevrolet Cobalt that feels like it could break down at any moment. I had a real internal struggle. On the interstate, I almost turned around a couple of times. This small journey would take up a significant portion of my day. I began to think about everything else that I could be doing, and tasks that I would now be falling behind on. The one thing that kept me going was the thought of Jesus. Jesus constantly went out of his way for the sake of others. I moved out of my own self-concern and stepped into the concern of John. The present situation has been close to hell on earth for him and his family. The very least I could do was deliver him a coffee to express love, support, care, and encouragement.

Thankfully, my not-so-trusty Cobalt got me there and back home safely. Just a few minutes ago John texted me and said, "Thanks again man, that was great, I needed that." Those words meant far more to me than the accomplishment of any work-related task would have meant to me. Was it convenient? No. Was that stepping out of self-concern? Yes. The way of Jesus is to go out of our way for the sake of others. Remember, we aren't just saved for our sake, but also for the sake of others. Self-concern told me to stay home and stay concerned about myself. Jesus told me to go out of my way.

Let's go back to Jacob and tie this all together. I'm confident that Jacob was empowered to step out of his narcissism because he embraced his new identity. Embracing your identity is the key to stepping out of your self-concern. Jacob embraced his new identity as "Israel", which, as you will remember, means "God prevails." Jacob committed to living a life on the side of God from this point forward. Israel developed into the people of God, and as I stated earlier, from the tribe of Judah in Israel, the Messiah came forward. "Israel" is connected to something beyond Jacob. When God declares that you are...

- His Child
- A New Creation
- His Workmanship
- A Kingdom Citizen

...you are now connected to something beyond yourself. You do not have those labels just for your sake so you can feel better about yourself. You have those labels so you can *embody* those labels for others, and hopefully one day invite them into the way of Jesus. As His Child, you show people the way to the father by your words and your actions. As a New Creation, you bring about restoration and life into other people's lives. As His Workmanship, you live in your purpose so that people can see they have also been created on purpose. As a Kingdom Citizen, you demonstrate what it means to respond to King Jesus over all other rulers and authorities, and how to live in freedom in a world of bondage. This is not just for you, it is for others!

The best way to truly step out of narcissism is to step into who God says you are, and live in that identity. Remember, people are not thinking about you as much as you think they are, and if by chance they are, who cares? Live above the pettiness of this world, and choose to live in a state of forgiveness, and a new label. God created you on purpose, for a purpose, and the purpose requires laying down your life for the sake of others. Sometimes laying down your life is as extreme as putting aside years of your life to invest in someone else. Most of the time it's as simple as going out of your way to show someone a personal act of love, like bringing them a cup of coffee.

Stop being consumed with what others might think about you.

Get over yourself.

What God says about you is far greater than what anyone else will say about you.

Before moving on to the next chapter, take a pause. Get up, grab another cup of coffee, go for a walk (or a short wander), but change your scenery as you pray about and consider the following questions:

Who do you need to forgive?

What label from Christ do you need to live in and live out?

Who have you been called to lay down your life for?

SIX

What Are You Aiming At?

Dr. Jordan B. Peterson is a clinical psychologist from Toronto who in recent years has had a rapidly growing influence. While some of Peteron's views may be considered controversial, one of his views I'm convinced is helpful for everyone is the call to "aim high." Peterson contends that the best thing we as humans can do is to aim our lives toward the highest possible good. And when you do, Peterson believes your world will shift itself around whatever it is you are aiming at.[37]

I believe Peterson's hypothesis to be true. Specifically, when what you are aiming at results in meaningful action, your life begins to move purposefully in that direction. Sometimes, the things in life that bring us down may only *be* bringing us down because our aim is off. If we adjust our aim, or focus our aim above the current circumstances, we may discover a new direction toward breaking out of the cycle that has been bringing us down.

---

37 https://www.youtube.com/watch?v=SmmPKLDX130

What are you aiming at?

What do your actions convey that you are aiming at?

⚔ Based on how you live your life, what would your closest friends or family say your life is aiming at?

Remember the definition of sin? It means to "miss the mark." Maybe the times in our lives when we feel like we aren't fulfilled is because we are aiming at the wrong target. Perhaps in those moments we are missing the mark. What if, whenever you choose not to aim at what God designed your life to aim at, you are missing the mark?

THE VILLAIN

Recently I have been wrestling with a theory. This particular theory is probably not unique to my own mind, but I admittedly have no recollection of hearing it elsewhere. The theory is that every person needs a villain. People love to have someone or something to push against. The villain is the thorn in your flesh, but the villain is also your motivation for getting out of bed in the morning. The villain can even bond you to a group or network of people as you work together to oppose this villain. The villain does not have to be a specific person, it can be a classification of people, a system, a force, or an agenda that you vehemently oppose.[38]

---

38 I plan to wrestle with this villain idea more in a future book. This particular topic could use more attention. For example, "What if you are born into a situation (your nationality, race, or economic class, for example) where you didn't choose your villain?" That's a good question worth further consideration.

I would like to contend that your villain is determining your aim. Whatever it is you are fighting against is influencing what you are aiming at. Therefore, the reason your life might be missing the mark is because your villain is not the true problem—it's just a symptom of a problem. Your villain may even be rooted in the very thing we are addressing: self-concern.

What is your greatest concern?

What issue in the world keeps you up at night?

What problem in the world do you actually want to be a part of solving?

What are you passionate about starting or stopping?

Answers to these types of questions will begin to define your villain, which in turn will determine your aim. What are you aiming at? What are you working toward? The following examples of villains are indicators that the aim of your life may not be toward your greatest potential:

- The person on social media who appears to be living a better life than you.
- The your manager or boss who can never seem to do anything right.
- The opposing political party that is "destroying" our country.
- The other company that just continues to outperfrom yours.
- Your sibling who always overachieves in life.

So much of this speaks to our desire to compete, our desire to win, our desire to be the victor. You may not think you're in any of these categories. Are you sure? Does anything similar to the above questions consume your conversations? Does anything similar to the above questions make you extremely disappointed or extremely happy? We have to adjust our aim. Maybe instead of competing with others in trivial pursuits we should be competing with the impossible. "When you're the best, you don't compare yourself against others; you compare yourself against the impossible."[39]

YOUNG JACOB VS. EXPERIENCED JACOB

Jacob's aim at a young age could be described as: "Look out for what is best for Jacob." The only villain getting in the way of what was best for Jacob in Jacob's mind would be Esau. Therefore, Jacob, with the help of his mother, stole both the birthright and the blessing. Jacob's actions can be associated with a faulty aim, and an immature choice of a villain sent Jacob's life into a complex trajectory. Maybe you have heard it said before, "You can either live twenty years of life or you can live the same year of your life twenty times over." Jacob may not have quite fit into that extreme, but he was close. This is what happens when you choose a low, selfish aim, and an unnecessary villain. Your life

---

39 Erwin Mcmanus, *The Way of the Warrior*, p.56.

develops into a cycle of seemingly the same thing over and over again. You begin to notice this cycle and you either:

Get bitter

Grow even more angry with your villain

Find a new villain but on the same level of aim

Live in denial

Break the cycle and aim higher!

Jacob eventually chose to aim higher, but it required him to listen to the voice of God. Remember all of the following circumstances?

- Jacob has a dream and God tells him he will bring him back to Bethel (Genesis 28:10-22).
- God speaks to Jacob, reminds him of the dream, and tells him to leave Laban twenty years later (Genesis 31:12-13).
- Jacob wrestles with God. God gives Jacob a new name. The new name gave Jacob a new meaning and purpose (Genesis 32:24-32).

As Jacob listened to the voice of God his life began to aim higher. By aiming high toward the call of God on his life Jacob was able to push against the villain of Laban and reconcile with Esau (who turned out to not be such a villain after all). When we step into the voice and the movement of God, the villains who appeared to be so treacherous begin to look different. The call of God on your life is the highest possible aim. As Jacob aimed high, he was able to press on and he did in fact make it back to Bethel just as God had promised.

> Then God said to Jacob, "Arise, go up to Bethel and live there, and make an altar there to God, who appeared to you when you fled from your brother Esau." So Jacob said to his household and to all who were with him, "Put away the foreign gods which are among you, and purify yourselves and change your garments; and let us arise and go up to Bethel, and I will make an altar there to God, who answered me in the day of my distress and has been with me wherever I have gone."[40]

Jacob recognized that even when his aim was off, God was with him wherever he went. This is why it is worth it for us to consider aiming at the highest good that God has called us to be. God is always with us, so we might as well function as if he is present. When we fix our aim without consideration of God, we are unnecessarily setting up a short-sighted aim. When we aim at the call of God on our lives, and the concern he has placed on our hearts, we engage with a villain that is far beyond the pettiness of this

---

40 Genesis 35:1-3

world. Jesus spoke of the great villain and refers to him as the "thief."

> The *thief* comes only to steal and kill and destroy; I came that they may have life, and have *it* abundantly.[41]

There is a villain in the spiritual world who is looking to take and destroy life. One of the ways he does this is getting your life to miss the mark by aiming at that which does not matter. When you aim at the call of God on your life you will experience life more abundantly. Jacob found this to be true. When Jacob's life was aimed only at his own good, his life was miserable. His life was headed toward destruction, and his actions destroyed his family. When Jacob's life became aimed at the call of God he was no longer identified with destruction of life, but he was given a new call to bring life. Jacob was given a new name which empowered him into a new vocation—to be the father of the twelve tribes who were called to give testimony to the surrounding world of the God who prevails. Jacob's son Judah would develop into the tribe of Judah through which the Messiah who gives abundant life would come forth! When Jacob chose to aim high, his life became a life that gave life instead of being aligned with the destroyer of life.

---

41 John 10:10

THE DISTRACTION OF AIMING LOW

When we aim low we quickly become consumed with self-concern. This means that the villain we are fighting is a villain that only affects us personally. Aiming low distracts us from fighting against the force of the true villain who is at work in the world to steal, kill, and destroy. When we aim low we will soon discover that the ultimate villain is stealing, killing, and destroying our very own souls because we have given into an endeavour that is not working for the greater good of humanity, or more importantly, the greater purpose of the kingdom of God. Instead we have given into an endeavour that is all about "me." If your aim is "me"-focused you are aiming low.

Aiming high in your individual life and aiming high with a group of like-minded people allows us to fight for life, and to fight against the one who is attempting to destroy life. The difficulty is the tension of doing good. We live in a world that makes it difficult to aim high and do the right thing. The people who are aiming their life in the direction of God's call are the people who truly make a difference because the aim is about the good of others. When our aim is off, when we miss the mark, self-concern comes creeping in. Do not become distracted in aiming low. Do not become discouraged in aiming high. The pursuit of that which is good is at times costly—but it's what you were designed to do, it's what we are called to do. Fight the distractions.

The tough truth is that when you choose to aim low in your everyday life you will inevitably play into the villain's destruction of your life. When you aim low you begin the destruction of your own soul, along with potentially bringing others down with you. When we aim high we bring life to others, we are brought into a greater concern for the world around us. I get it though. You have grievances in life:

Your difficult spouse

Your unruly children

Your mundane job

Your disloyal friends

Your obnoxious parents

All of these things can be a distraction to aim low, and they focus on your feelings in the immediate situation instead of focusing on your call to the greater situation at hand. I'm continually inspired by people who have found a way to aim high, having discovered God's purpose where God has placed them. You are not where you are by accident. Look at where you are in your life and aim your life in the pursuit of God. Through that aim you will begin to discover a greater concern right where you are.

I could give many examples of people aiming high in the apparent normalcy of everyday life, but I have one example that particularly spoke to me recently. This story is from my friend Kaylyn. Kaylyn works for Of The Sea, a marketing company here in Buffalo. At the beginning of the COVID-19 pandemic in early 2020, Kaylyn made a critical decision to aim high and find God's purpose for her in the middle of a difficult season. Kaylyn started a movement called "Fueling the Frontlines with Coffee." I will let her tell her story…

> "Fueling" was born out of a conversation we had as a team back before quarantine even started. Then we began to watch as businesses shut down, the economy collapsed, and friends and family members lost their jobs. Erik challenged each of us to think of a way we could give back to the Buffalo community as a team.
>
> A few weeks later, I was on Instagram (yes, this is true) and scrolled past a print I had seen before. It was an art print of Coffee Cups of New York City. In the past when I had seen it I searched the web for a version in Buffalo but never found it. If there is one thing I've missed during quarantine, it's sitting in a local coffee shop. Once again, I did a quick Google search. Still nothing popped up. And then a lightbulb went off. I thought, what if we at Of the Sea created a version of the print which included Buffalo coffee shops. Then we'd take the proceeds and give them back to those featured on the print.
>
> The next morning, on our daily Zoom call, I presented the idea to the team. They jumped on board

and helped take the idea even further. We decided that the proceeds from the sale of the poster would be given to the local coffee shops, and then, in turn, they would provide coffee to local frontline workers and first responders. And of course, all donors would receive a Coffee Cups of Buffalo print. We contacted local graphic designer Sarah Hofheins to design the print and Rory Allen from ZoomBUFFALO to help print the poster. We created the landing page, social media, reached out to each coffee shop to get them involved, and launched the campaign Fueling the Frontlines with Coffee.

On the first day we raised $5,000. We were blown away. I never expected it to catch on this quickly. But the Buffalo community never ceases to amaze me. It's one of my favorite things about this city and I will forever brag about it. We have each others' backs.

The reason behind the campaign was that every day our healthcare workers and first responders were leaving the safety of their homes and putting themselves in harm's way in order to save lives. We wanted to recognize the sacrifice they made and support them while they battled on the front lines. But my favorite part of this campaign is that it not only benefits frontline workers and first responders during the pandemic, but it supports the local coffee shops I have grown to love so much who had no choice but to stop business as they knew it.

Now that the campaign has slowed and we are closing it out, the Buffalo community raised $40,000 (all of which went to the local coffee shops featured on the print) and 12,000 cups of coffee were provided to local frontline workers and first responders. I have heard so many amazing stories during this campaign. But one that stands out is when we asked the coffee truck Bean Bastard to share what being a part of this campaign meant to them in a social media post. The owners shared that this campaign saved their business. A week before quarantine, both of them quit their full-time jobs to go full time with their passion. And then a pandemic hit. (I cried when I heard this, but maybe don't mention that). They told us the campaign helped relieve some of the stress of owning a business during a global pandemic. And I thought, this is what it's about. This is why we did this. It made the stress, anxiety, and tears (yes, more tears) worth it knowing that we made a tiny difference in these people's lives. As a brand manager of an advertising agency, sometimes my work doesn't feel meaningful or purposeful. But this campaign was life giving. I'm so grateful I got to be a part of this, and thankful that the Buffalo community showed up.

This is what means to aim high. To aim at the highest possible good is to aim at what God has called you to. God is the one who is good and all that is good comes from him, therefore, to aim at his purpose for you is how we orient our lives to aim at what is good. Kaylyn could have bought into the lie that she is "just a brand manager." Her aim in that mindset would have been at small things like:

Working to get a raise

Working to build a resume

Working to get through the day

Each of those thoughts is legitimate, but they were not her ultimate focus. Don't allow your ultimate aim to be on such small, self-concerned things. Remember there is a villain at work in the world, and he desires to destroy life. He will even use real-world events like COVID-19 to steal hope from people. Kaylyn didn't give into that story of hopelessness, instead she aimed high. Kaylyn fixated her aim on the one who gives life, and from that she was able to bring life to others. When we aim high, we defeat the agenda of the great villain who is trying to destroy life.

In aiming high, Jacob became Israel. In aiming high, Kaylyn stepped into God's purpose in a difficult season. Don't give into a low aim. Pursue the highest good that is God himself and his purpose for your life. Take up your cross and follow him. Pursue the upward call in Christ! AIM HIGH!

Not that I have already obtained it or have already become perfect, but I press on so that I may lay hold of that for which also I was laid hold of by Christ Jesus. Brethren, I do not regard myself as having laid hold of it yet; but one thing I do: forgetting what lies behind and reaching forward to what lies ahead, *I press on toward the goal for the prize of the upward call* of God in Christ Jesus.[42]

---

42 Philippians 3:12-14

SEVEN

Genesis: Part One

Move Forward

Up to this point we have covered the major themes of our friend Jacob. We have to remember that Jacob's story happens within the context of a book. This book is called *Genesis*, which literally means "origin." There is something within this book that speaks to the origin, or the beginning, of humanity. I would be remiss not to look at Jacob's story through the full lens of the book of Genesis. Therefore, I intend to do just that within Chapters Seven, Eight, and Nine. This is by no means a detailed commentary on the book of Genesis, but there are a few concepts from the book of Genesis that I would like to explore in these three chapters. The first concept (Chapter Seven) I want to explore is, "Breaking away from the familiar." The second concept (Chapter Eight) is, "When your journey chooses you." The third and final concept (Chapter Nine) asks the question, "What does it mean to be human?"

THE FAMILIAR

Our favorite stories involve a character who steps into the unfamiliar. For example, in *Star Wars: A New Hope* (1977), Luke Skywalker, who grew up in a seemingly safe place, steps into the unknown. Luke was a farmer who lived with his aunt and his uncle. When his aunt and uncle are killed, he decides to step into the unknown of going against the evil Empire with the help of an old Jedi by the name of Obi-Wan Kenobi. We all wish we could be like Luke. We all have dreams of stepping out of the familiar and into the unknown of a greater purpose.

Obi-Wan had been on great adventures before, he had a knowledge of the galaxy. Obi-Wan also demonstrated to Luke that he had knowledge of a greater power called the Force. It was much easier for Luke to step into the unknown because he had a mentor who had been there before, and was willing to go with him. I wonder how many of us would be more willing to step into the unknown, to step out of the familiar, and step into a greater concern if we had a mentor figure with us who went before us?

What if we did have a figure who went before us? What if we had someone who was with us wherever we went? What if when you stepped into the unknown you had someone leading the way who did not see this space as "unknown"?

THE JOURNEY

Remember the passage that got this entire thing started? "Then Jacob went on his journey."[43] A journey typically requires stepping into the unfamiliar. This is a theme that we see over and over again in the Genesis story. It's not solely Jacobs' story. We read of a similar story with Noah, Jacob's grandfather Abraham, Jacob's grandmother Sarah, and Jacob's father Isaac.

God called Noah: *"Make for yourself an ark of gopher wood; you shall make the ark with rooms, and shall cover it inside and out with pitch."*[44]

God called Abraham: "Go forth from your country, and from your relatives and from your father's house, *to the land which I will show you;"*[45]

God called Sarah: So Sarah *conceived and bore a son* to Abraham in his old age, at the appointed time of which God had spoken to him.[46]

---

43 Genesis 29:1a

44 Genesis 6:14

45 Genesis 12:1

46 Genesis 21:2

God called Isaac: "Now there was a famine in the land, besides the previous famine that had occurred in the days of Abraham. So Isaac went to Gerar, to Abimelech king of the Philistines. The Lord appeared to him and said, "Do not go down to Egypt; *stay in the land of which I shall tell you.*"[47]

Each of these characters is facing a different type of unknown. Noah was building an Ark in a world that had never seen a boat or a flood. Yet he moved forward to the call of God on his life. Sometimes stepping out of the familiar will require taking actions that appear to be nonsensical to others. Abraham followed the call of God to go to "the land which I will show you." Talk about a risk! Abraham didn't even know where he was going. Sorry, no Google maps for Abraham. Abraham's wife Sarah had Isaac. This doesn't seem unfamiliar at the surface level. Women have babies. This was unfamiliar because Sarah was over ninety years old when she had Isaac. Will we step into the unfamiliarity of bringing life into the world, even when it seems physically impossible? Isaac's journey is interesting because he was called to stay. The call to stay may have seemed a great risk for Isaac since he was raised by a father who was always on the move. Isaac's journey is a reminder to some us that

---

47 Genesis 26:1-2

maybe your call right now is to stay. Sometimes we have an addiction to change that is fed by a commitment issue. In this case, the greatest potential risk for you is to stay. Staying could be your unknown, because you have never stayed anywhere longer than six months. The journey looks different for all of us, but it always entails an element of the unfamiliar.

Each of these characters stepped into their version of the unknown based on the call of God. If you journey beyond self-concern, if you journey into a place where you aim high, if you journey into God's call on your life, you must be ready for the unknown. Look at how the author of a book called Hebrews remembers Noah, Abraham, Sarah, Isaac, and Jacob:

> By faith Noah, being warned by God about things *not yet seen*, in reverence prepared an ark for the salvation of his household, by which he condemned the world, and became an heir of the righteousness which is according to faith. By faith Abraham, when he was called, obeyed by going out to a place *which he was to receive* for an inheritance; and he went out, *not knowing where he was going*. By faith he *lived as an alien in the land of promise*, as in a foreign land, dwelling in tents with Isaac and Jacob, fellow heirs of the

same promise; *for he was looking for the city* which has foundations, whose architect and builder is God. By faith even Sarah herself *received ability to conceive, even beyond the proper time of life*, since she considered Him faithful who had promised. Therefore there was born even of one man, and him as good as dead at that, as many descendants as the stars of heaven in number, and innumerable as the sand which is by the seashore.[48]

By faith Isaac *blessed* Jacob and Esau, even regarding things to come. By faith Jacob, as he was dying, *blessed* each of the sons of Joseph, and worshiped, leaning on the top of his staff. [49]

Faith is the key concept. They had faith in the one who went before them, and therefore they were able to step into the unknown. The book of Genesis has an underlying theme of God's call for humanity to step into the unknown for the good of others. The journey is a call to be a blessing to others. The unknown can be frightening. Like Abraham you may not know where you are going,

---

48 Hebrews 11:7-12
49 Hebrews 11:20-21

and you may feel like an alien, a foreigner. If your journey is in the direction of being a blessing to others, rooted in a call from God, you can know that you are headed in the right direction.

FIGHTING THE FAMILIAR

We are all at war internally with that which is familiar. Even if you're not a person who appreciates routines you probably appreciate some level of predictability. I know far too many people who are missing out on their God-given potential because they choose the journey of the familiar over the journey of faith. Familiarity, even in a less-favorable situation, brings a level of comfortability. Predictability can become an idol, something else we give our appreciation or attention to, that drags you down.

can it be Both Familiar faith?

What I have discovered is that there are a small portion of people who feel as if they are thriving in life. There are a small portion of people who are on the opposite end of the spectrum who just absolutely hate their life. Then there seems to be a huge portion in between who feel that life is just mundane. The mundane group doesn't recognize the opportunities that God has placed in front of them to call them into a greater journey. Self-concern places us in a cycle of mediocrity and the routine, a place of disenchantment and indifference. The catastrophe of life is when you choose not to step out of the familiar because of self-concern. Concerns like:

- If I move to pursue my purpose will I make friends?
- What if I start a company and fail?
- What if people mock me if I produce the content I have been working on?
- That company appears to have a much better work environment than the horrible place I currently work at, but what if I take the job, it doesn't work out, and they fire me? I might as well stay.

The two final concerns that hold most people back and keep them rooted in the idol of self-concern:

- What if I pursue _____ and don't make money?
- What will people think of me?

The goal should not be to make money. If your sole goal is to make money then you will experience failure. You might succeed in making money, but you will sacrifice so much relationally it will be for nothing. And if you only consider what people think about you then you must accept a life of self-concern in the cycle of the mundane. People will always misunderstand you. Just because other people don't see the vision and have never stepped into the unknown doesn't mean you should allow them to hold you back. On the other hand if your goal is to make a positive difference in the world then you will work harder than everyone else and never give up. You will also discover great relationships as people are compelled to join in with a noble cause.

Let me be clear. I'm not encouraging irresponsibility. I'm not saying drop everything and do whatever you want. Responsibility, hard work, and planning are required for the journey ahead. When we began to plan the launch of New Story Church we told God that we would not start moving forward until he sent us another couple to work with us. Within a month God sent us the Friedmans and we put together a two-year plan. Yes! Two years! Two years of praying, prepping, and much more. Then we raised $100,000+ in nine months. Stepping into the unknown of God's call will connect you to your passion, but your passion requires hard work. Maybe you have heard the saying, "*Do what you love and you will never work a day in your life.*" We have warped that saying into "Do what you love and you will never *have* to work a day in your life." Hate to break it to you, but pursuing the unknown will probably take far more work then what you're doing right now. The work is part of the reward. You have been given a gift, a talent, an idea, an ability that exists for others. Pursue God's purpose. Lean into the unknown of the call of God on your life.

In the life and ministry of Jesus, Jesus told a lot of parables. Parables are essentially stories that were not necessarily historically true, but they have truth in them, specifically in regards to the human experience. Jesus told these parables to stimulate thought on how humanity could step into the call of God. Jesus told a very powerful parable that speaks to some of the struggle we have in pursuing the unknown. Please read this parable very closely. I have even used a more simplified translation of the parable so that we can have a more clear understanding.

"The kingdom of heaven is like a man who was going to another place for a visit. Before he left, he talked with his servants. The man told them to take care of his things while he was gone. He decided how much each servant would be able to care for. He gave one servant five bags of money. He gave another servant two bags of money. And he gave a third servant one bag of money. Then the man left. The servant who got five bags went quickly to invest the money. The five bags of money earned five more. It was the same with the servant who had two bags of money. He invested the money and earned two more. *But the servant who got one bag of money went out and dug a hole in the ground. Then he hid his master's money in the hole.*

"After a long time the master came home. He asked the servants what they did with his money. The servant who got five bags of money brought five more bags to the master. The servant said, 'Master, you trusted me to care for five bags of money. So I used your five bags to earn five more.' The master answered, 'You did well. You are a good servant who can be trusted. You did well with small things. So I will let you care for much greater things. Come and share my happiness with me.'

"Then the servant who got two bags of money came to the master. The servant said, 'Master, you gave me two bags of money to care for. So I used your two bags to earn two more.' The master answered, 'You did well. You are a good servant who can be trusted. You did well with small things. So I will let you care for much greater things. Come and share my happiness with me.'

"Then the servant who got one bag of money came to the master. The servant said, 'Master, I knew that you were a hard man. You harvest things you did not plant. You gather crops where you did not sow any seed. So I was afraid. I went and hid your money in the ground. Here is the bag of money you gave

How would the master feel if he was lost?

?

me.' The master answered, 'You are a bad and lazy servant! You say you knew that I harvest things I did not plant, and that I gather crops where I did not sow any seed? So you should have put my money in the bank. Then, when I came home, I would get my money back with interest.'

"So the master told his other servants, 'Take the bag of money from that servant and give it to the servant who has ten bags of money. Everyone who uses what he has will get more. He will have much more than he needs. But the one who does not use what he has will have everything taken away from him.' Then the master said, 'Throw that useless servant outside, into the darkness! There people will cry and grind their teeth with pain.'"[50]

There are many layers to a parable. For our purposes I want to peel back one particular layer. The guys with five bags of money and two bags of money had a lot more to lose, yet they still took a risk into the unknown. The guy with one bag of money had the least to lose but he was the most afraid to take a risk. How often do we get caught in

---

50   Matthew 25:14-30 ICB

the cycle of the man with one bag? We don't really have that much to lose, and as a result we assume that we also don't have much to gain, so we become paralyzed and do nothing. We just hold on to what we have, and we do nothing.

The man with one bag had a wrong view of the master, and he had a wrong view of what the master had given him. He thought the master would be upset if he took the risk out of the familiar. The master gave him the money so that he would do something with it, he wanted him to step out of the familiar. ⟵ *unclear*

In the Bible, these bags of money are called "talents." A talent was a measurement of a certain amount of money. God gifted to each of these men a certain number of talents to use, to invest, to grow. The word talent became the very word we use today to describe our own God-given gifts and abilities that are meant for the benefit of others, even more so when we apply them, practice them, and improve upon them. The more we grow in our talent, be it dancing, music, acting, or business, teaching, or leadership, people will be blessed by the increase in our talent. God gave you your talents, gifts, and abilities so that you could step out of the familiar. God has a call on your life and he wants you to use it, not hide it and bury it like the man in our parable did with the talent, the bag of money, that was given to him.

Notice what happened with the men who used the money provided to them? They made more money. This story is not so much about the stewardship of money as it is about the stewardship of life. What have you done with the life that God has given you? God has given you a purpose, a telent, that will build up others into *their* purpose. The money multiplied because their master gave them something good. When you pursue God's call in faith you will make a difference because our good God has given you good abilities, good gifts, good talents that will make a difference. Don't become buried in the familiar. Don't give into the lie that you have nothing to offer. God has given you something special. He's provided you with a purpose. You've been gifted a talent. Step into the unknown.

FAITH TO MOVE FORWARD

Let's return to Obi-Wan Kenobi. Remember the whole idea of how Luke had the confidence to move forward into the unknown because he had a mentor with him that had knowledge of the journey? Noah, Abraham, Sarah, Isaac, Jacob, and, yes, YOU have access to someone who has gone before you. Someone who made a way for you! Remember the words of the writer of Hebrews? "By faith…." The characters we looked at had faith in a God who had control over all things, and who spoke truth over their life. By faith in God you can move forward into your calling. Faith is the key that will pull us out of the familiar. We read later on in the book of Exodus with the story of Moses that God is a

God who goes before his people: "The Lord is the one who *goes ahead of you*; He will be with you. He will not fail you or forsake you. Do not fear or be dismayed."[51] God goes before us! The unfamiliar to us is familiar to him.

In our modern times we now connect to God through Jesus (John 14:6). When we follow Jesus we can step into the unknown because by the power of the Holy Spirit he is with us wherever we go (1 Corinthians 6:19). Just as Jesus called a bunch of sinners, tax collectors, fisherman, pharisees and many others to follow him into the unfamiliar, he is calling each of us to do the same. But here is the good news. Jesus never changes: "Jesus Christ is the same yesterday, today, and forever."[52] Therefore, we can know that he truly will be with us in whatever unfamiliar space we step into, just as he was with Paul, Peter, Stephen, Mary, and so many others. In Jesus we can have a confident faith that allows us to fight the familiar.

Don't get caught in the mundane. Don't get caught in the ordinary. Don't bury what God has given you. The story of Genesis is the story of the beginning of all things. From the beginning, God has been *calling* humanity into a journey and *leading* humanity into that journey. God's design is for you to step into a journey of the unfamiliar. Let's have the faith to move into the space of the unfamiliar.

---

51 Deuteronomy 31:8

52 Hebrews 13:8

This is our time to be pioneers by journeying into the unfamiliar for the good of others!

God said to Abraham before his journey:

And I will make you a great nation,

And *I will bless you,*

And make your name great;

And *so you shall be a blessing;*[53]

When you by faith step into the unfamiliar journey God has for you, you will be blessed, but your blessing is given so you can *be* a blessing. Respond to the call. Accept the blessing of following Jesus so that you can be a blessing! Have the faith to move forward!

---

53 Genesis 12:2

EIGHT

Genesis: Part Two

When the Journey chooses you

If you have some familiarity with the book of Genesis you know that there are some prominent characters that we did not mention in the last chapter. One of these characters is Joseph, one of Jacob's sons. Jacob had twelve sons, but Joseph receives a significant amount of stage time in the book of Genesis. Joseph will be the focus of this chapter because there is something very unique about the journey of Joseph. Noah, Abraham, Sarah, Isaac, and Jacob each in some way or another had a choice in regards to their journey. Joseph, on the other hand, didn't really have a choice. Joseph's journey chose him. What do you do when your journey chooses you?

This is a powerful question for those who have been a victim of horrible circumstances in their life. What do you do when:

- Your parents split up at a young age?
- Your father leaves because he doesn't want the responsibility of raising you, so you never meet your dad?
- Your spouse is unfaithful in marriage?
- Your dream job fires you?
- You and your spouse cannot seem to have children?
- Your closest friends turn on you in a difficult season?
- You trusted someone in a position of authority and they used that trust to abuse you or manipulate you?
- Your kids become adults and want nothing to do with you?
- You unexpectedly lose a loved one?
- You were picked on, neglected, or bullied your entire childhood?
- You are misunderstood or accused of something that you didn't do, but now there are life consequences for the accusations that have been brought against you?
- You grew up in a neighborhood where you were exposed to things that you should have never been exposed to such a young age?

What do you do when the journey chooses you, especially when the journey is filled with such sorrow, pain,

THE JOURNEY OF JOSEPH

Jacob had twelve sons, but Joseph was his favorite. Jacob loved Joseph so much that he made a special coat for him. Joseph's brothers were not fond of him for a number of reasons. They obviously didn't like that he was the favorite, but you could also make the argument that Joseph was potentially a tattle tale, and potentially a little full of himself. At one point in his youth, Joseph had a dream that implied all of his brothers would one day bow down to him. He then felt compelled to share that with his brothers. Joseph's brothers had enough. They decided to take matters into their own hands and they sold their brother into slavery. Upon selling their brother into slavery they reported to their father that Joseph was dead.

Joseph is eventually purchased by a high-ranking Egyptian official by the name of Potiphar. Joseph finds favor with Potiphar, and Potiphar elevates Joseph's position in the household. Potiphar's wife finds Joseph attractive—she wants to have some fun in the bedroom with Joseph, if you know what I mean—but Joseph refuses because he doesn't want to dishonor Potiphar. As Joseph runs away from Potipher's wife, she grabs a piece of his clothing and screams! Joseph is falsely accused of attempting to take advantage of Potiphar's wife and he ends up in prison.

While in prison, the chief jailer becomes very fond of Joseph, so he is treated well in prison. Joseph is given the responsibility of being over all of the prisoners. During this time, the Pharaoh's baker and cupbearer are sent to prison. One night, they both have dreams, and Joseph interprets them: he tells the cupbearer that his dream means that he will be found innocent and restored to his position, and he tells the baker that his dream means that he will be found guilty and be hung on a tree. I'm sure the baker was wishing at that moment that he had not asked about his dream! Joseph asks the cupbearer to remember him when he is set free and to make a request to Pharaoh for his freedom. Unfortunately, the cupbearer forgets.

But two years later, Pharaoh has a dream. Not a single one of Pharaoh's wise men could interpret it. The cupbearer suddenly recalls Joseph and his abilities and mentions him to Pharaoh. Released from prison and brought before Pharaoh, Joseph tells Pharaoh that his dream is from God himself, who is revealing that there will be seven years of abundance for Egypt, followed by seven years of famine. Pharoah is most impressed, and he appoints Joseph to be the second-most-powerful man in all of Egypt, second only to himself.

We will stop there for now.

Yes, Joseph did become the second-most-powerful man in Egypt.

But two quick things:

1. He did not choose that journey

2. How do you go from being sold into slavery and later being wrongly accused and thrown into prison to beccoming the second-most-powerful man in Egypt? *How???*

I imagine you have been in this space before. That space where the journey appears to be choosing you, and the choice or choices that the journey has made for you do not appear to be in your favor. I've been in this space before, not to the extent that Joseph was, but we all can relate to an unexpected hurt, tragedy, or pain in our journey that seems to be changing the trajectory of our journey. When we look at Joseph, I believe there are three consistent traits of who he was as a person that empowered him with the faith to move forward—even when the journey that was chosen for him did not seem to be working in his favor.

TRAIT #1: JOSEPH'S RESPONSE

Joseph's brother's sold him into slavery. A woman accused him of trying to make a move on her and he did no such thing. A man in jail said he would remember Joseph when he was free but forgot for two years. These incidents are not to be taken lightly. Especially the concept of his brothers selling him into slavery. Joseph never had an opportunity to choose the journey of his life. In fact, it seemed the journey of his life was to follow in his father's footsteps; he was being groomed to take over the family business. He'd had dreams implying great things lay in store for him. And all at once, he was betrayed by his brothers, shackled and sold. Joseph was seventeen years old when he was sold into slavery. Imagine the various types of emotional scars a circumstance like that could leave a person with:

If you cannot trust your own family then who can you trust?

If your brothers will betray you then who else will betray you?

If you're destined to never see your family again, what does the concept of family even mean to you? Is it even possible to find or create a new family?

Abandonment.

Loss.

Disappointment.

Betrayal.

Anger.

Bitterness.

Hate.

All of the above questions and feelings seem pretty valid based on what Joseph's brothers did to him. I imagine if you have been betrayed by a family member you have probably experienced those emotions or asked one of those questions. I am sure Joseph did as well, but we never read that he expressed them because he did not allow those emotions and questions to prevail.

Joseph demonstrates the importance of our response in our journey. When your journey chooses you, and it's a dark path like Joseph's, you will need to go through some type of recovery process. Whether that recovery is with a mentor, a counselor, in a group, or through your own spiritual journey, there comes a time when you have to own your response. This ancient story still speaks so powerfully today because the tragedy of a journey that has been chosen for you still speaks to many people. You might be reading this right now and you are looking at your life saying, "I didn't choose this journey." That's understandable.

Don't allow a circumstance, a person, or a situation to rob you of pursuing the journey that God has for you. Joseph refused to allow a bad circumstance to own the journey of his life. *The villain who comes to steal, kill, and destroy wants to convince you that you have been robbed of your freedom to choose.* The journey up to this point may have been chosen for you, but you cannot allow the circumstances within the journey to own you. Joseph never allowed his circumstances to own him. The prevailing response of Joseph was to determine how he could best pursue God even in an uncertain situation. Joseph didn't allow the villain of life to rob his ability to choose. Joseph chose to pursue God no matter the circumstances, which meant that ultimately

God was in control of his journey. We will see the power of God at work in Joseph's life once we see where Joseph's life ends up, but more of that to come later.

When Joseph's brother's sold him into slavery they ripped off the coat that Joseph's father had made for him. Joseph would have no physical reminder of his past life. I wonder at times if, in his darkest moments, he wondered if his past with his father Jacob was even a reality.

Joseph's brothers sold him to the Ishmaelites, and who in turn sold him to Potiphar. Potiphar recognized that God was with Joseph (Genesis 39:3). When Joseph was wrongly accused and ended up in prison he was placed in charge of the prison (Genesis 39:22). Joseph waited patiently in prison, and years later when he was finally brought before Pharaoh he gave all of the credit to God for the interpretation of dreams (Genesis 41:16). Joseph always had a prevailing response: "In light of my situation how can I best show people who God is?"

I'm confident that at times Joseph felt like a victim, but he never chose to live as a victim. There is a big difference between being a victim by definition and living as a victim. If you are a victim there is freedom, healing, recovery, and victory accessible to you in Christ. As I mentioned earlier, healing occurs in a different process for different people. This is a critical part of your journey. When your journey chooses you and the path gets dark, will you allow yourself to be told that you are nothing more than a victim? Or will you seek the help necessary to move forward? Will you step into the way of Jesus and find that in him you can step into a place of victory?

Joseph had the proper response because He was confident in the victory that only his God could provide. And when you truly understand the eternal victory you have in Christ your response will never be the response of a victim. The victory that Jesus gives you actually empowers you to tell your story to bring victory to others. Victory is saying, "No matter what the great villain tries, I will not relinquish my power to choose." Christ has given you the power to move forward and to choose your response. Don't allow your journey to dictate your response. Instead, allow the all-powerful, all-loving, all-knowing, all-VICTORIOUS presence of Christ determine your response. When you journey from a place of victory, the journey will never successfully choose you. "*[B]ut thanks be to God, who gives us the victory through our Lord Jesus Christ.*"[54]

TRAIT #2: JOSEPH'S RESOLVE

We have all been at a place where we say we believe one thing but our actions don't quite align with what we claim to believe. I'm not always as concerned with what people say they believe. I'm more attentive to people's actions, because actions are a more accurate depiction of what

---

54 1 Corinthians 15:57

someone truly believes in their heart. This applies a level of accountability to me and to my own words as I seek to hold myself to the same standard. What you do is a declaration of what you believe.

Joseph's actions made it very evident to those around him that he believed that God was with him no matter the circumstance. Joseph didn't just claim belief in God. He truly believed, and the actions which resulted from his belief, both in good times and in bad times, resonated with those who were close to him. Joseph was unwavering in his resolve. He appeared to be good with God, at all times, in all things...and people noticed.

> **Potiphar's Perspective:** The *Lord was with Joseph*, so he became a successful man. And he was in the house of his master, the Egyptian. Now *his master saw that the Lord was with him* and how the Lord caused *all that he did* to prosper in his hand. [55]

> **In Prison:** But the Lord was with Joseph and extended kindness to him, and *gave him favor in the sight of the chief jailer*. The chief jailer committed to Joseph's charge all the prisoners who were in the jail; so that whatever was done

---

55 Genesis 39:2-3

there, he was responsible for it. The chief jailer did not supervise anything under Joseph's charge because *the Lord was with him; and whatever he did, the Lord made to prosper.*[56]

Pharaoh's Perspective: So Pharaoh said to Joseph, *"Since God has informed you of all this*, there is no one so discerning and wise as you are. You shall be over my house, and according to your command all my people shall do homage; only in the throne I will be greater than you."*[57]

When Joseph was in a good season with Potiphar and with Pharoah it was noticeable that the Lord was with him. When Joseph was in a dark season in prison it was noticeable that the Lord was with him. Notice that the author also states that the Lord was with Joseph in "all that he did" and "whatever he did." That means that Joseph was never sitting around doing nothing. Sometimes we function in the idea that to reflect the manifestation of God in our lives people must see us praying, singing, reading scripture, or participating in some type of religious activity. While those practices are good, and they do point to our belief

---

56 Genesis 39:21-23
57 Genesis 41:39- 40

in God, sometimes the best way to give testimony to our belief is through what we do *outside* of our religious activities—in the home, at work, through our finances, or with our friends.

In the good times we don't just celebrate and sing all of the time. In the dark times we won't just lock ourselves in our bedroom and pray all day every day. There will be moments for those actions to occur, but there is more to what we are designed to be as humans. We have a unique opportunity not to be paralyzed by the good or the bad. We can function well in both if we have resolved in our hearts that God is somehow at work in all of it.

Recognizing God in the good times means that you do praise him, you do celebrate him, and you do speak of his goodness. But you also continue working hard at whatever it is he has called you to do because other people must experience that same goodness. If you stop working in the good times you potentially surrender the opportunity to function from a place of faith. When you stop working in the good times you begin to fall into a place of complacency. There is still work to be done even in the good times.

In the bad times we must press on and know that the Lord is with us. Your story will be the catalyst to help somebody else move forward in their story. If you stop working, if you stop functioning, if you stop believing in the goodness of God, then the darkness will just get darker. The villain wants to convince you that the darkness is all encompassing and there is no way out. If you buy into this lie you will aim low, and be consumed by the darkness of your own self-concern. What if God doesn't want to deliver you immediately *from* the bad circumstance, but he wants to do something *in you* in the midst of the bad circumstance? I don't want to downplay the difficulties of life, but I do want to let you know that God sees you, God hears you, and he is working. Joseph had that resolve in his heart, and as a result he was able to act out the belief of his heart even in difficult times. Joseph knew that God was *always* working in his life.

God never stops working, so we never should either. A testimony of belief is not a testimony of stagnate spiritual disciplines. A testimony of belief is best displayed in what we do. Joseph resolved in his heart to act on his belief in God no matter what happened to him. Allow God to shape you in your circumstances instead of allowing your circumstances to shape you. Imagine what our communities would look like if, no matter the situation, we resolved in our hearts to act on our belief in a good God who is at work?

May we all remember the words of James the brother of Jesus:

> Consider it *all joy*, my brethren, when you encounter various trials, knowing that the testing of your faith produces endurance. And

let endurance have its perfect result, so that you may be perfect and complete, lacking in nothing.[58]

Count it all Joy!
God is at work!
Therefore, you can keep working!
Endure!
Persevere!
Resolve in your heart, soul, and mind that God is good!

TRAIT #3: JOSEPH'S RESPONSIBILITY

During the seven years of famine that Joseph told Pharaoh would come, Joseph's brothers make the journey from Canaan to Egypt to obtain some food for their family. Joseph is in charge of food distribution and he recognizes his brothers when they arrive, but his brothers do not recognize him. It has been over twenty years since they sold their brother into slavery. It's not hard to imagine that they couldn't recognize him, especially considering the ancient context. They didn't have any photos or old videos to remember his appearance. He is no longer that kid brother, he's a full-grown man. Joseph is dressed as an Egyptian, poised like an Egyptian, speaking Egyptian. It would be more surprising if they *did* recognize him.

---

58 James 1:2-4

Joseph decides to play some games with his brothers before revealing himself to them. One of the games includes sending them back home with the mandate to return to Egypt with their youngest brother Benjamin, holding one of the brothers hostage until their return. Benjamin and Joseph shared the same mother, so it makes sense as to why Joseph would want to see Benjamin, not to mention that considering his own fate at their hands, he was probably concerned for Benjamin's welfare. His brothers return home and tell their father that they must return to Egypt with Benjamin, but Jacob does not like that option. Joseph's brothers finally convince their father to let Benjamin go, and they travel back to Egypt. Joseph continues to play more games with them, leaving them puzzled that someone in such a high position should take such a particular interest in them. Finally, unable to restrain himself any more, Joseph reveals to them who he is.

Then Joseph said to his brothers, "I am Joseph! Is my father still alive?" But his brothers could not answer him, for they were dismayed at his presence.

Then Joseph said to his brothers, "Please come closer to me." And they came closer. And he said, "I am your brother Joseph, whom you sold into Egypt. Now do not be grieved or angry with yourselves, because

you sold me here, *for God sent me before you
to preserve life.* [59]

Reunited and it feels so good! Remember that dream that Joseph had that his brothers would one day bow to him? Turn's out he was right. Unfortunately, for that dream to come true Joseph's brothers had to act out the extreme betrayal of selling Joseph into slavery. Think for just a minute about the position of power that Joseph finds himself in. He is the second-most-powerful man in the world. He could do literally whatever he wants to punish his brothers. He lost out on twenty-two years of life with his family because of his brothers! Sure, he has a lot of possessions and influence now, but you can't buy back time. All of the cards are in his hand. And with such power over the ones who sold him into slavery, what does he choose to do? He tells them to go home and come back with their dad, their families, and everything they own. Joseph is going to provide for them a special place in Egypt to live (Genesis 45:9-10).

This begs the question. How do you view the responsibility you have been given? Joseph used his responsibility as an opportunity to forgive instead of an opportunity to enact vengeance. When we have a resolve that a good God is at work in everything that happens to us, we set ourselves

---

59 Genesis 45:3-5

up as people who can forgive even the worst offenses. When the journey chooses us, we can quickly step into God's journey for us when we choose to forgive. Joseph used his responsibility as the second-most-powerful man in the world as an opportunity to forgive.

Joseph did not allow his "good" and "prosperous" season to be a time to become complacent or to kick up his feet and not care about the world. Notice he said to his brothers, "God sent me here to preserve life." Our goal for our life should not be to kick up our feet and do nothing. Our goal should be to stay so connected to our good God that no matter the season we never stop working for the good of others. The following words of Joseph are stunning:

> *God sent me before you* to preserve for you a remnant in the earth, and to keep you alive by a great deliverance. Now, therefore, *it was not you who sent me here, but God*; and He has made me a father to Pharaoh and lord of all his household and ruler over all the land of Egypt. [60]

See what he did there? While Joseph's journey "happened to him," he never allowed his journey to own him or have authority over him. Joseph chose to understand

---

60 Genesis 45:7-8

that his journey was initiated by, ordained by God. Joseph's journey didn't have authority over him, what his brothers did to him didn't have authority over him, but it was God who had authority over his life. When God has ownership over your life you can confidently know that every part of your journey is a "sent" place by God. Give God the keys to your life. Allow God to show you your responsibility in the good seasons and the dark seasons. Don't allow someone or something to have authority over you. When you give someone or something authority over you, you lose your sense of responsibility, which robs you of your opportunity to live. Your God-given responsibility is your God-given right to live freely on the journey he has ordained for you!

If you are or have at one time been a helpless victim like Joseph, when I say "responsibility" I'm *NOT* implying that you should take responsibility for what happened to you. Whatever reprehensible thing happened to you is *NOT* your fault. To further clarify, I'm encouraging you that through your healing process I want you to discover that you do in fact have value! Therefore, you have the privilege of responsibility, as an image-bearer of God, to add value to wherever God has placed you! Don't allow a person, a circumstance, or a situation to rob you of that value and responsibility that has been given to you by God. God has sent you and has given you value and responsibility. Don't allow the "villain" to tell you otherwise. Don't allow the villain to win his game of stealing, killing, and destroying.

Years later, after Joseph's brothers have settled into the land Joseph provided for them, Jacob passes away, and Joseph's brothers become nervous that Joseph may turn on them. They assume that his kindness toward them all of these years was only for the sake of their father. Joseph's brothers approach him in trepidation.

> Then his brothers also came and fell down before him and said, "Behold, we are your servants." But Joseph said to them, "Do not be afraid, for am I in God's place? As for you, you meant evil against me, but *God meant it for good in order to bring about this present result, to preserve many people alive.* So therefore, do not be afraid; *I will provide for you and your little ones.*" So he comforted them and spoke kindly to them.[61]

I cannot emphasize enough that the goal of life is not to "retire" or "kick back and relax." I'm not anti-rest, but I am anti the "idol of rest," as though perpetual rest in our lives was something to expect and seek after in this life. Joseph was at the best place possible in his life, but he still recognized the responsibility given to him by God to preserve lives and to take care of his extended family. If your goal is

---

61 Genesis 50:18-20

to "retire and do nothing with no responsibility," you will find that it leads to a place of overwhelming self-concern that will eventually become isolating, lonely, and dark. The idol of "doing nothing" is one the sneakiest ways that the villain will destroy your life.

We must recognize that every season has responsibility. Every season calls us to take up our cross. Rejoice in your responsibility. Your responsibility speaks to our Good God's design for you, the design of value that he has placed on your life. God has given you responsibility because just as he gave to the world, he has placed something in you to give to the world. Don't hold back what God has given you. Step into your power to choose. Step into your responsibility to go for the good of others, to move forward wherever God has placed you.

What do you do when the journey chooses you?

Respond from a place of victory in Christ!

Resolve to reflect the goodness of God!

Never allow someone or something to rob you of the *Responsibility* that only God can truly give you!

NINE

Genesis: Part Three

What does it mean to be human?

In 2008, an extraordinary band by the name of The Killers released a song called "Human." The chorus of the song repeatedly asked the question, "Are we human? Or are we dancer?" People who listened to the song, including myself, didn't quite understand either the grammar or the essence of the question. The lead singer of The Killers, Brandon Flowers, explained the lyrics in an interview with MTV. [62] "It's taken from a quote by [author Hunter S.] Thompson. ... 'We're raising a generation of dancers,' and I took it and ran. I guess it bothers people that it's not grammatically correct, but I think I'm allowed to do whatever I want," he laughed."[63] This message—that we are raising a generation

---

62 Anybody reading this remember when MTV was relevant??

63 http://www.mtv.com/news/1598299/killers-brandon-flowers-stands-behind-human-chorus-feathery-jacket/

of dancers—implies that we have a generation who may have lost the ability to think for themselves and will just fall in line with whatever the current "wave" is. When we look at the state of the world today, I think we could all agree this is a compelling theory.

To go along with Flower's analogy, we are individuals meant to be more than just "dancer." But at times, we choose to live beneath our calling by just falling into line without question. What is compelling as we consider the intent of humanity within Genesis is that we discover that we were not intended to just "fall in line." Humanity has been created on purpose, by a good God for a good purpose.

Genesis chapter 1 begins with God creating everything. God looks at everything that he created and seven times he declares it "good." Genesis chapter 2 in some ways recounts Genesis chapter 1, but in a different way. There are theories surrounding how to interpret the two accounts, but we can explore those theories in a different book at a different time. I want to look at specifically what each account says about humanity. Are humans being created with an intent? Or are humans just dancers meant to fall in line with a system?

> Then God said, "Let Us *make man in Our image, according to Our likeness;* and let them *rule* over the fish of the sea and over the birds of the sky and over the cattle and *over all*

the earth, and over every creeping thing that creeps on the earth." *God created man in His own image, in the image of God He created him; male and female He created them*. God blessed them; and God said to them, *"Be fruitful and multiply, and fill the earth, and subdue it; and rule over the fish of the sea and over the birds of the sky and over every living thing that moves on the earth."* Then God said, "Behold, I have given you every plant yielding seed that is on the surface of all the earth, and every tree which has fruit yielding seed; it shall be food for you; and to every beast of the earth and to every bird of the sky and to everything that moves on the earth which has life, I have given every green plant for food"; and it was so.[64]

Then the Lord God took the man and put him into the garden of Eden to *cultivate it and keep it*. The Lord God commanded the man, saying, *"From any tree of the garden you may eat freely; but from the tree of the knowledge of good and evil you shall not eat, for in the day that you eat from it you will surely*

---

64 Genesis 1:26-30

die." Then the Lord God said, "It is *not good* for the man to be *alone*; I will make him a helper suitable for him." Out of the ground the Lord God formed every beast of the field and every bird of the sky, and brought them to the man to see what he would call them; and whatever the man called a living crea- ture, that was its name. The man gave names to all the cattle, and to the birds of the sky, and to every beast of the field, but for Adam there was not found a helper suitable for him. So the Lord God caused a deep sleep to fall upon the man, and he slept; then He took one of his ribs and closed up the flesh at that place. The Lord God fashioned into a woman the rib which He had taken from the man, and brought her to the man. The man said, "This is now bone of my bones, And flesh of my flesh; She shall be called Woman. Because she was taken out of Man."[65]

This is the beginning of the journey. The beginning of the story where God has created humanity to function within a context of a "greater concern." Humanity has been designed to work for the concern of God in the world. By

---

65 Genesis 2:15-23

reflecting the image of God, humanity has been created to bring the very presence of God to this earth. These two passages speak so powerfully to the potential and the capability of humanity. What does all of this mean for the journey that God has sent you on?

RETELLING THE STORY

In Chapter Five I addressed a narcissistic view of faith that has been popularized in our modern context. There is a hint of truth in the story that is told by modern westernized evangelicalism. The truth is that all have sinned—nobody is exempt from this reality. But while all humans have sinned, all humans have also been created in the image of God. There are two parts of humanity that speak to our relationship with God:

- All humans being sinners speaks to each human's need for healing from God.
- All humans being created in the image of God speaks to each human's individual potential.

When we only focus on the "sin" part, we create a mindset that we are "good for nothing." Sin is serious and I do not intend to downplay it. Sin is so serious that Jesus died on a cross for it. In Genesis 1 and 2, sin has not yet entered the world, therefore, humanity fits into the "good" that God declares over his creation. As image bearers of

God that goodness is still in all of humanity. Sin holds us back from doing the greatest good or the best form of good. This helps to answer the question, "How can someone who doesn't know God do something good?" Whether that goodness is as simple as an act of kindness or starting a business that makes a positive difference in your community, the reality is that the act of good is a reflection of the image of God that has been placed on your life.

If you didn't grow up in faith this thought process probably makes sense to you. "Humans are capable of evil (sin) and they're capable of good (the image of God)." If you grew up in faith you may be short circuiting right now. You are probably asking, "If you believe humanity is good then why did Jesus have to die to pay for our sin?" Humanity's essence has been imprinted by a good God, but our essence has also been fractured by sin. Therefore, for us to experience the fullest potential of the good we have been created for we must know Jesus so that we can be cleansed of all unrighteousness (1 John 1:9). The work of Jesus at the cross is the only thing which can heal the fracture of sin and restore our capacity to realize the purpose for the good we have all been called to. The capacity of good within every human speaks to the mark of a good creator on our lives, but that goodness will always be fractured until we come to know the one who truly is good. Walking in the way of Jesus allows us to experience the fullest potential of the goodness we have been created for and the way of Jesus allows us to experience God's goodness for all of eternity.

Adam and Eve (the first two humans in Genesis 1 and 2) fractured the good image of God for humanity when they made the choice to eat from the tree that God told them not to eat from, the tree that would bring death. The tree was known as the tree of the "knowledge of good and evil." As soon as they ate from the tree they were exposed to both good and evil, because to intentionally disobey God's directive *was* evil. Evil became their choice, and sin, and with it death, entered the world. Beforehand, they only knew that which is good as they functioned in a relationship with a good God. When we tell the story of God and humanity we must start here. Humans are created by a good God in his image. That goodness is still within us but it has been fractured by sin. Thankfully Jesus paid for that sin on the cross and in following Jesus we are brought into our greatest potential to work for the good of others. All humans can do "good" things and work for the "good" of others, but our greatest potential to do those things is found in Jesus because he restores humanity's relationship with the one who is good!

Notice when God created Adam and Eve he gave them responsibility to rule (Genesis 1:28) and to cultivate the garden (Genesis 2:15). God has given humanity an innate desire to be responsible, to do good, to make a difference, to work! This responsibility in the garden is working for the good of creation that humanity has been placed in. The call of God to humanity to work hard for the good of creation still exists today. Humanity working, moving, making a difference, speaks to the image of God that has been placed on our lives.

Telling the story this way speaks to God's value and desire for humanity. God desires humanity to function in our fullest potential for good, which is working toward good for others and the good of creation as a whole. This moves our story out of narcissism and self-concern. This moves your story, my story, and the story of humanity into a recognition that we have been created for something beyond ourselves, a greater concern.

All humans are created in the image of God and therefore have value. At the same time, all humans are sinners in need of a savior. This is the best possible anthropology because it acknowledges the inherent value of the individual along with a call to recognize that no individual is perfect.

If you are "just a sinner" then you have no intent beyond yourself, you have no value. If you are created in the "image of God" then your life speaks to something beyond you, your life speaks to a responsibility that has been given to you by God! When we tell the story this way (the way it was intended to be told) we see how humanity has been created to work for God's greater concern for the world. Adam and Eve's opportunity to live with a good God in the good garden, and do good work in the good garden, is the original intent for humanity. That original intent for humanity can be *fully* restored in Christ. The Spirit of God within Christ followers will renew our hearts and minds to go for the good of others just as Christ did.

We get after God's greater concern for the world when we go for the good of others!

Humanity has value as image-bearers of God.

That value speaks to a good God!

GOD'S GREATER CONCERN

God's greatest concern is that we know him. God's concern is expressed and displayed in God going to the great length of sending his very son so that we can be brought into relationship with him. Paul expresses God's concern in his letter to Timothy when he says that God desires for "all men to be saved."[66]

Jesus is the image of the invisible God (Colossians 1:15), therefore, in coming to know God through Jesus, the good image of God is being fully restored within us. Jesus was fully God and fully man. When we study the life of Jesus in the Gospels we see what it means to be truly human. In Jesus we see how the good work of God can interact with creation to restore the goodness of creation.

What does this mean in regards to the good that we are called to work for? If God's greatest concern is for humanity

---

66 1 Timothy 2:4

to know him, that means that we are truly operating within the context of the greatest good when everything we do is for the purpose of bringing people to a saving knowledge of Jesus. We must pray for the same heart that the apostle Paul had when he expressed that the church of Colossae be presented as "complete in Christ." The highest and truest expression of good is to do whatever you're doing with the desire of bringing people to Jesus. When that becomes the concern of your good work, then your concern is truly overlapping with God's concern.

"Whatever you do in word or deed, do all in the name of the Lord Jesus, giving thanks through Him to God the Father."[67]

JOURNEYING TOGETHER

In Genesis 2:18, God declares that it is not good for man to be alone. This is one of those verses that speaks to marriage, companionship, and our relationships. I'm going to take more of a 30,000-foot view on this particular verse, and not dive into the specifics. Before the fracture of sin, God declared that human's needed relationships. We all enjoy stories of the lone hero who breaks the rules and overcomes all of the odds without any assistance. But when we look at our contemporary heroes we recognize that they never truly did it alone:

---

67 Colossians 3:17

Batman: Alfred

Robin

Batgirl

Nightwing

Harry Potter: Hermione

Ron Weasley

Dumbledore

Frodo: Sam

Merry & Pippin

Gandalf

Aragorn

Luke Skywalker: Leia

Han Solo

Yoda

Obi-Wan

None of our heroes accomplished great things alone, they always had great people surrounding them. We need other people. Humanity is not designed to do life alone. We need faithful people in our lives who we can work together with. Being connected to other humans also helps us to stay away from self-concern. When you know other people, and you are doing life with others, you begin to see beyond your own context.

As we have planted a church, we have needed our friends Neil, Lindsay, Joy, and Aaron. We have been able to rely on them, and they have been to rely on us. Starting a church is not an easy thing to do, but doing it with others allows us to carry the weight together. Doing it with other people also allows us to connect with other people. We have a team in our church called the "Story Team," and we have groups called "Story Groups." In these communities we continue to build New Story Church, but we also carry the weight of life together and celebrate the victories of life together.

You are not designed to do life alone. Humanity is not designed to do life alone. Maybe someone has hurt you or broke your trust in the past. Don't allow what one person has done to you taint all relationships for you. That is exactly what the villain wants. If the villain can convince you to isolate yourself he can get closer to winning his game of stealing, killing, and destroying, because the only voice you hear in isolation is your own. Relationships are not easy, but this is my charge to you to fight for good, healthy, consistent, deep relationships. "[A]nd let us consider how to stimulate one another to love and good deeds, not forsaking our own assembling together, as is the habit of some, but encouraging one another; and all the more as you see the day drawing near."[68]

---

68 Hebrews 10:24-25

GENESIS: PART THREE

LIMITATIONS

We sometimes have a perception that God has a lot that he wants us to avoid. Depending on the narrative that you have received about God you may think God is all about saying "no." In God's initial intent for humanity, he actually had more things they *could* do as opposed to things they *couldn't* do. God was all about the green light.

Green light:
- Be Fruitful and Multiply
- Fill the earth
- Subdue the earth
- Rule over the fish of the sea and the birds of the sky
- Rule over every living thing
- Eat
- Cultivate and keep the garden

Red Light:
- Don't eat from the tree of knowledge of good and evil

In fact, *everything* that Adam and Eve did or could do was to the glory of God. Play, sleep, swim, make, build, plant, kiss, draw, relax, or stare up at the clouds, everything was a fulfillment of God's purpose in their lives. There was one, and only one, restriction in all of their lives. It was abstract. Set aside. Off in the middle of the garden. It was the singular way they could make a choice to do God's will, or refuse God's will. They really were free. Virtually without limitation.

God isn't as into limitations as we may have previously assumed. If you read the Scriptures you read in the Old Testament Law in the book of Leviticus that God has many red lights. Why the change? Well there are many contextual reasons. Here the two main, general reasons for all of the red lights in Leviticus:

1. Sin is now in the world. God wants his people to avoid sin.

2. Some of the Levitical commands were contextual. God wanted his people to not be like the pagan nations, so he commanded that his people not to do certain things like get tattoos (Leviticus 19:28), because the nations of that time would typically get tattoos as a part of their worship of pagan gods. God didn't want his people to be associated with pagan nations. That particular law no longer applies today; it was contextual. In fact, when Jesus returns he will have a tattoo on his thigh (Revelation 19:16).

Now we can jump back to the Genesis story. God initially placed one limitation on humanity: Don't eat the fruit of the tree of the knowledge of good and evil. Unfortunately, Adam and Eve gave in and broke this one limitation, they just had to eat from the tree. The breaking of that limitation brought sin into the world. This brings us to Adam and Eve's two sons. Cain and Abel. Cain and Abel both make sacrifices to God. There is something wrong with Cain's sacrifice. Something about his attitude, his heart, in bringing his gift to God. Cain is keenly aware that God is pleased with his brother Abel's sacrifice and not his. Driven by jealousy and motivated by a hardened heart, Cain kills his brother Abel. What does this have to do with limitations? Remember the name of the tree? The tree of knowledge of *good* and *evil.*

Adam and Eve are now parents, and their older son killed their younger son. This is the knowledge of good and evil. In the garden they only knew good, the garden was the place where a good God rested with his creation. Now they have knowledge of both good and evil. In Cain's actions we see the potential of humanity's evil, and we see the potential of evil that can happen to you. God's limitation was not arbitrary. God's limitation was from a good God for the good of his creation. God was attempting to protect humanity from the potential of the action of evil, and the pain and hurt of someone else's evil actions. The fall of humanity not only makes humans capable of evil, but it also opens up the possibility of evil that can happen to you. Adam and Eve broke one limitation and released this whirlwind.

Once again, here is another reason why the way of Jesus is so compelling. If we were to truly be honest with ourselves, we are all aware of the evil we are capable of. Likewise, we are aware of the evil that is capable of happening to us. Look no further than social media, the news, and anywhere that humans have a platform and you will humanity's capacity for evil.

Consider the way of Jesus.

The ethic of Jesus

This is My commandment, that you love one another, just as I have loved you.[69]

The presence of Jesus

These things I have spoken to you, so that in Me you may have peace. In the world you have tribulation, but take courage; I have overcome the world."[70]

Jesus has one limitation that falls under one commandment. His one commandment is to love others as he has loved you. If you want to dive into more specificity of what that life looks like then read the biographical accounts of the life of Jesus: Matthew, Mark, Luke and John. Within

---

69   John 15:12
70   John 16:33

those biographies you will see this commandment played out in the life of Jesus through his teaching and his actions, but this is ultimately the one limitation. This is how we avoid the evil that we are capable of: to love others as Jesus loved us. Jesus loved with sacrificial, committed, honest, truth-filled, undefiled, and life-changing love. Jesus loved with a love that put others before himself. When we follow this one commandment to walk in the way of Jesus we will begin to move toward a greater concern, toward the good that we are designed to do.

The limitations that Jesus refers to as "sin" are what lead us to a place of not loving others the way Jesus loved others. Sin says, "How can I best love myself?" which eventually leads to evil, and self-concern. The way of Jesus says, "How can I best love others?"

The presence of Jesus is all too real as well. Jesus gives his disciples a warning that he gives us today. We will face tribulation and trouble in this world. There is evil that can happen to us. How do we endure the evil that happens to us? Cling to Jesus. Jesus has overcome the world. Jesus has overcome the worst curse of sin: death. Jesus overcame death, and therefore he has the power to carry you through whatever evil and darkness you are facing. Embrace the limitation of following Jesus. The limitation of Jesus leads to life! Jesus is *for* you! Jesus will pull you toward the good of others and he will comfort you in your tribulation so you don't get carried into the black hole of the villain.

UNIQUELY HUMAN

Within our humanity there is a uniqueness to each of us. We are each individuals with our own gifts, preferences, abilities, and styles. The Psalmist declares the recognition of his individuality when he declares, "I will give thanks to You, for *I am fearfully and wonderfully made.*"[71] Later on in the New Testament the apostle Paul recognizes the differences of individuals when writing about the body of Christ, "Now you are Christ's body, and *individually* members of it."[72] While we all need one another within the context of a group, we all each have something that makes us uniquely human. I have observed that there are three general barriers that will at times hold people back from being uniquely human.

1. Family Barriers

When it came to independence and discovering who I was as an individual, I was fortunate that I had amazing parents. My parents knew that I felt called to ministry, and as soon I graduated high school they allowed me to pack up my car and move seven hours away to Buffalo, New York. My parents are not wealthy, so they didn't send me away with a bunch of money and they didn't have any emergency money put away in case I ran into any issues. They

---

71 Psalm 139:14a

72 1 Corinthians 12:27

had confidence in me as an eighteen year old to journey off into the world and make decisions. I thought this was normal, but as I have gained more life experience I have realized that this was not so normal.

I'm beyond thankful that my parents allowed me to pack up my car and pursue my dream and call for my life. I was going to work at a camp for $10,000 a year and I had no plan to go to college at the time, but they supported me. You may think that sounds crazy, but it allowed me to learn about how to live life. I discovered who I was, what I value, how to be responsible, and how to make decisions for myself. This experience of trekking off on my own allowed me to discover who I am as an individual.

Too many people have the development of their individuality delayed because their family doesn't trust them to be an adult. I'm not a parent ,so I'm not suggesting "how to parent" per se, but I would like parents to consider allowing their kids to make more adult decisions at a younger age.[73] I have worked with high school students and college students for a number of years and it becomes pretty apparent which kids will go further faster. Oftentimes they are the kids whose parents allow them their independence and the ability to explore. When you can explore and *own*

---

73 For all of you rebellious high school students, while it is important at your age to learn how to make your own decisions, you are still under your parents' care and responsibility. Greater life decisions will be yours to make when you are older. Sorry guys, you don't have a license to argue with your parents.

your "success" and "failure" you begin to discover who you have uniquely been created to be as a human.

If you're reading this and you're in your early twenties and you're looking for some direction in life, my question for you is, "How far away have you journeyed from your roots?" This doesn't have to be physically journeying to another location, it can be merely conceptually journeying. Have you exposed yourself to ideas that are different than the ones you grew up with? Have you met new people? Don't become so comfortable with the standard of your roots that you don't develop as a human. Take a risk! When I initially didn't want to go to college[74] it definitely made my parents a little nervous, but they allowed me to own that decision. If God is leading you to make a decision but you know that decision may ruffle some feathers in your family, that's okay! Break the norm!

Challenge the status quo!

Go for it!

When your life is in God's hands he will work it out. Let God shape you into who he has created you to be.

2. Cultural Barriers

I was recently listening to an interview with the hilarious Nick Offerman. If you're not familiar with who Nick

---

74 In case you are curious, I have since attended college and obtained a couple of degrees.

Offerman is, you may better know him as the character he portrays on the show *Parks and Recreation*, Ron Swanson. If you don't know who Ron Swanson is, I pity you. In the interview, Offerman talked a lot about his growing up years. Offerman was raised in a small town where the majority of people worked blue collar jobs that require manual labor. When Offerman was in high school he began to develop his desire to be an actor or a musician. Nobody in his town ever really pursued either of those careers.

Offerman's guidance counselor, his family, and others attempted to gently steer him in a different direction. His guidance counselor knew of one person from their town who pursued a life in the music world and was now a professor at a small college teaching music. That was the ceiling of what people in his town could accomplish in pursuing the arts. Offerman chose to break the cultural barrier that had been placed around him and pursued a career in acting. Thank God he did! Because of his courage to break the cultural expectation we now have Ron Swanson!

The unique call that God has on your life as an individual may cause you to break a cultural norm. There may not be anybody that you know who is doing what it is that you feel God has called you to do. That's okay. It's also okay if you know a lot of people who know what it is that you feel called to do. It doesn't have to be obscure to be a call from God, but if it is obscure, that's okay! Don't allow the cultural barrier to hold you back. Let God do what only God can do! Let God shape you as the individual he created you to be and break the cultural expectations that are around you!

3. Conformist Barriers

I've been a part of a number of groups that have been led by strong leaders. When I say strong leaders I mean people of vision, charisma, and direction. One of the hardest things for me to watch is for a human to step into a group bursting with potential, but for that potential to become minimized because the person gives into the average standard of the group and that person conforms. I have watched this happen one too many times, and I'm not even thirty years old yet. I'm not advocating for disobedience within a group (which I can be known for) or for breaking the norm just to break it (which I can also be known for 😂). To be truly human means you are *a great follower* but *not a conformist*. When you have a strong leader, more often than not the standard of the group becomes an imitation of the strong leader. This imitation becomes a conformity that limits the individual, which ultimately limits the group. Sometimes the leader doesn't even recognize that this is happening. The subconscious standard of the group can rob you of your unique calling.

I've witnessed too many humans miss out on their unique calling because of the comfort of conformity. Most humans who do this don't even notice when it's happening to them. To give into the standard behavior of the group can be strongly driven by self-concern. You don't want to step into your uniqueness because you're concerned about what people might think. Here are some things to ask yourself.

- Have my predominant mannerisms begun to reflect the leader of the group?
- Has my vocabulary developed into words or phrases that are predominantly used by the leader of the group?
- When was the last time I confronted someone in the group or disagreed with them?
- When was the last time I politely questioned my boss or reported on an issue?
- When was the last time I brought a new idea to our group?
- Am I being innovative? What am I bringing to the team that nobody else brings?

Your answers to those questions may reflect whether you have started down the road of losing your individuality. Yes, we as humans need one another, but we should also celebrate our differences. When God called the prophet

Jeremiah (years after the book of Genesis) he made some very bold claims about Jeremiah's humanity.

> "Before I formed you in the womb I knew you, And before you were born I consecrated you; I have appointed you a prophet to the nations."[75]

God knew Jeremiah before he formed him in the womb.

God consecrated (set apart) Jeremiah in a special role as a prophet to the nations. If anyone ever tells you they are a prophet to Israel or a prophet to the nations I would be wary. Actually, you should probably correct them or RUN! That role no longer exists. But the essence of what God says to Jeremiah still rings true for every human today.

Before you were in the womb God knew you! God has set you apart and appointed you for a specific purpose. Your general purpose is to reflect his image, rule over the earth, and work!! Within that general purpose there is a specific purpose. Don't allow the pressure of a group to rob you of humanity and the calling that God has given you. A good group, a secure group, a Godly group, will elevate your differences and celebrate them! Confidently step into who God has uniquely created you to be!

---

75 Jeremiah 1:5

GOD'S GENEROSITY

"Then God said, 'Let Us make man in Our image, according to Our likeness.'"[76] The creator of all things, the one who spoke the entire universe into existence, allows humans to have his image. The generosity of God is truly stunning. In our world we are obsessed with "branding." Some brands are so particular they only want a certain "type" of person representing their brand, which obviously makes sense for marketing and consumer appeal. But God doesn't look at you in this way. God allows you, God allows me, God allows every human to bear his image. The one who is over all things is not very concerned about his brand. God is a generous God who gives his creation his very image.

As you go on your journey remember that you have been created in the image of God. God has spoken promises over your life, and he sent Jesus so that you can step into the life God designed you for. We are all lost, we are all looking for purpose. Jesus is the only one who came for us to show us the way to life (John 14:6). Every other guru, leader, ruler, or kinging says, "Come to me," "Buy my books," "Buy tickets," "Do _____ for me." Jesus said, "I'm coming for you," and he did. God generously gave humanity his image, and in Christ's generous sacrifice on the cross God made it possible for the fractured image to be restored.

---

76 Genesis 1:26a

To live a life outside of the context of self-concern is to live a life of generosity. To live a life for the good of others is to truly be generous with your time, your finances, and your resources. Live in the greater concern of God for the world. Don't walk around without purpose hoping that the people in your life will find Jesus. Do what Jesus did for you and bring Jesus to the people in your life. How do you bring Jesus to the people around you? The answer to that question is found in another question. How do you love people the way that Christ has loved you?

Jesus did what Adam could not do.

Jesus is the true picture of what it means to be human.

Don't give into the narrative for humanity that the world is selling.

Don't give into the subconscious standard of the group.

Don't be a dancer.

Be a human!

TEN

Back to Jacob

Before we embarked on the journey of planting a church I held various jobs in what you would call "vocational ministry."[77] In one of my earlier roles, I recall in my hiring process my soon-to-be boss gave me a document detailing my new position, and that it would require "forty hours a week." We had multiple follow-up conversations in regards to what exactly that meant, and he would always caution me that people would ask a lot from me, but that I didn't need to exceed my forty hours a week. I grew to really like this rhythm. It was in some ways liberating, to either not respond to people or just say "no" if I was asked to do something that exceeded my scheduled hours.

Kim was working in the same place at the time, and she was also instructed not to exceed her forty hours each week. We were loving life. We came home before five o'clock, we

---

77 This is just a fancy way of saying I was paid to work in ministry.

watched a lot of Netflix and had a lot of "me" time or "us" time. We were living the dream, right?

In the spring of 2017, Kim and I took a vacation. As a part of our vacation we went to a two-day conference at Elevation Church called "Inside Elevation." We were blown away! A spark was reignited in us that reminded us of the call we had both received to go into ministry when we were in high school.[78] When people see a church like Elevation they assume that it's just a bunch of flash, big lights, and shallow spirituality. That myth could not be further from the truth. The commitment that their staff has to working hard, praying hard, and reaching people far from God is challenging and inspiring. If you want to see how real and raw ministry is executed in a way that truly connects with people, go visit Elevation Church. I have never seen a team that is more committed to ensuring that people's lives are truly transformed by Jesus.

Through our experience at Inside Elevation, God began to reveal to Kim and me a complacency that had developed in our hearts. We began to realize that we were not being driven by the command of Jesus to go into all the earth,

---

78 I was raised in Virginia. In my senior year of high school I felt called to plant a church. I graduated high school in June of 2012 and moved to Buffalo. I met my wife that summer. Kim is from the Buffalo area. When she was in high school she felt God told her she would one day marry a pastor. We were friends for a couple of years, and started dating in 2014. The rest is history.

but we were driven by the goal of reaching our forty hours for the week then having our time to relax. Complacency had taken over our hearts, and complacency is just another doorway to self-concern. When you're complacent you will not go out of your way for the good of others.

Following that experience, we committed to be no longer driven by a forty-hour work week, complacency, and comfort. We made a decision to lay down our preferences for the good of others. That is what Jesus chose to do, so we were going to do the same.[79] Complacency has no room in the life that God has called us to. We have been called to act, to sacrifice, to venture off the path of convenience. Read the biographies of the life of Jesus in the Gospels. His life was marked by sacrifice. If we are following Jesus, why would our lives look any different? It breaks my heart to see people who are following Jesus who have bought into the same complacency that I had bought into. You were created with a call on your life, don't give into complacency.

The thought of fighting complacency brings me back to my fascination with Jacob. "Then Jacob went on his journey...."[80] Though Jacob was sometimes driven by the wrong motives, he was never complacent. Jacob was always

---

79 Kim was much better than me at making this transition. Kim can stay focused on her commitments no matter what is going on around her. If I get frustrated, I quickly retreat into self-concern. I have learned from her in this area to not allow my circumstances to dictate my drive.

80 Genesis 29:1a

on the move. Yes, Jacob struggled with self-concern, but it was never a self-concern that was driven by complacency. I think too many Christians become afraid that, like Jacob, their ambition might be distorted, so they choose complacency over action. We have a tendency to look at a life like Jacob's (especially the early years) and run from the opportunity of a journey. Instead, we should look at the journey of Jacob's life and use it as a guide to help us make better decisions in our own journey. Decisions that aim high. We are meant to journey, and a journey requires movement. Movement wars against complacency.

FAREWELL JACOB

At the end of Jacob's life he has moved into a greater concern. Jacob has his new name, "Israel," and he is living in the reality of that name. Israel, the beacon of hope who declares "the God who prevails." Jacob is old. He has every justification to just relax and do nothing. In some people's eyes, he has a right to be complacent in this season. Yet, Jacob takes one last journey to reunite with his son Joseph, and once reunited with his long lost son, he still chooses to give. Jacob is elderly, he has lived a full life. Nobody would fault him for refusing to give more. But Jacob still chooses to give, even when he doesn't have much left.

> Then Jacob summoned his sons and said,
> "Assemble yourselves that I may tell you what

will befall you in the days to come. Gather together and hear, O sons of Jacob; And listen to Israel your father.[81]

Jacob proceeds to prophesy over each of his sons. Jacob even prophecies in regards to the Messiah, Jesus (Genesis 49:10). Jacob went from being a man who stole blessings to a man who gave blessings. Jacob continues to give, and he is speaking into the future by prophesying over his sons. When we move out of self-concern into God's greater concern for the world we step into building God's future for the world. God's greater concern is that we would extend his Kingdom work—for people to be saved, for humanity to know God, and to love others as Jesus loved us—which is building the ideal future that he has for his creation. Jacob was willing to do this before breathing his last breath. Don't give into complacency, which implies you should just receive blessings. We were created to give blessings! Step into the journey of blessing others that God designed for you. What is stopping you from stepping into the journey God has designed you for?

CREATING GOD'S FUTURE

We obviously live at a different time than when our friend Jacob lived. One of the major differences is the way in

---

81 Genesis 49:1-2

which God is moving in the world. In Jacob's time, God the Father would speak audibly to someone like Jacob and call him into various endeavours. We now live in a post-resurrection time.

Jesus came two thousand years ago, died on a cross for you and for me, rose from the grave, and then ascended into Heaven. Once Christ ascended, the Holy Spirit was sent, and now anyone who follows Jesus is given the Holy Spirit. If you are following the way of Jesus you no longer have to wait for the audible voice of God like Jacob did because the Spirit of the living God lives inside of you. That means wherever you go, God goes. The Spirit is restoring you to your original intent, as a true image-bearer of God. The Spirit is empowering you, and every other follower of Jesus, to go on a journey of God's greater concern for the world that builds his desired future for his people.

When Jesus rose from the dead, he had a new, resurrected body. I believe that this resurrected body is a reflection of the resurrected bodies we will one day have in the *future*. Paul says in Romans that the same Spirit of the resurrected Christ currently dwells with us (Romans 8:11). That means that the Holy Spirit dwelling in us is a part of the *future* dwelling in us. The Holy Spirit is renewing our hearts and minds to bring about the *future* that God intends in the world and for the world. This is why Jesus taught us to pray, "Your kingdom come. Your will be done,

On earth as it is in heaven."[82] When we live in the power of the Holy Spirit we are declaring to the world that Jesus is King. We are participating in bringing about God's Kingdom, God's will on earth as it is in Heaven. We don't pray that prayer in hopes of God one day becoming King. He *already is* King. The first words out of Jesus' mouth in Mark's biography is that the Kingdom of God is here. Jesus may not yet be publicly recognized as King (he one day will be), but right now in the present, as followers of Jesus, we build the future by living the reality that we already know to be true, that his Kingdom is active and his will is at work in our lives here on earth, just as his Kingdom and will are at work in Heaven. This is why we should step into God's concern. When we step into God's concern for the world, we are stepping into his eternal Kingdom work.

In 1 Corinthians 15, Paul gives a wonderful explanation of the gospel, the work of the resurrection, and the resurrected life. At the end of the chapter, Paul makes a powerful statement that inspires us to step into God's concern for the world. "Therefore, my beloved brethren, be steadfast, immovable, always abounding in the work of the Lord, knowing that your *toil is not in vain* in the Lord."[83] Your toil, your work, is not in vain. What you do for the Lord in the power of the Spirit is not useless, it has

---

82 Matthew 6:10

83 1 Corinthians 15:58

substance, it builds the future. We will turn to the words of the great Scholar N.T. Wright for further understanding of this passage:

How does believing in the future resurrection lead to getting on with work in the present? Quite straightforwardly. The point of the resurrection, as Paul has been arguing throughout the letter, is that *the present bodily life is not valueless just because it will die*. God will raise it to new life. What you do with your body in the present matters because God has a great future in store for it. And if this applies to ethics, as in 1 Corinthians 6, it certainly also applies to the various vocations to which God's people are called. What you *do* in the present—by painting, preaching, singing, sewing, praying, teaching, building hospitals, digging wells, campaigning for justice, writing poems, caring for the needy, loving your neighbor as yourself—*will last into God's future*. These activities are not simply ways of making the present life a little less beastly, a little more bearable, until the day when we leave it behind altogether (as the hymn so mistakenly puts it, "Until that day when all the blest to endless rest are called away"). They are part of what we may call *building for God's Kingdom*.[84]

---

84   N.T. Wright, *Surprised by Hope*, Harper Collins, 2008. p.192-193.

He made my point.

How could we possibly fall into complacency when we are building God's future?

TAKE A JOURNEY

We started with two thoughts: Jacob's Journey, and exploring what it means to be free from self-concern. I hope that from Jacob's journey you saw the power of stepping out of self-concern and into God's call. I hope that through Jacob you saw the power of redemption, and the importance of wrestling with God. Jacob journeyed out of self-concern and stepped into God's concern.

To be concerned is not inherently bad. The question is, "What type of concern are you being driven by?" My hope is that after reading this you wouldn't only step into a journey of greater concern, but you would also step into following Jesus. The voice of the Spirit of God in your life will always keep you on track to step into the future of God's concern for the world. There will be daily struggles and distractions calling you into self-concern, self-preservation, and complacency, and all these things pull you away from being truly human. Do not allow the villain who intends to steal, kill, and destroy pull you onto a path that is beneath your capabilities and your created intention. Step into the way of Jesus, the way of being human, the way of bringing about God's will on earth as it is in Heaven.

May God's will become your will.

God's will is the only lasting will.

Don't settle for complacency. Complacency only assumes that this is it. This is all there is to be content with. There is nothing more to work for. Complacency cares for now, not the future, and certainly not God's intended future.

Follow the Holy Spirit into the way of Jesus.

The way of Jesus is the journey into the future.

> "For I have come down from heaven, not to do My own will, but the will of Him who sent Me."[85]

You have been sent to do the will of God in the world, to journey into the future!

The concern of the future is a greater concern!

Enjoy the Journey!

---

85 John 6:38

Made in the USA
Middletown, DE
13 January 2021